Believe, Believe, Believe

James Henry Lincoln Sr.

Copyright © 2024 **J and G Publication**

All rights reserved. No part of this publication may be reproduced, distributed, or transmitted in any form or by any means, including photocopying, recording, or other electronic or mechanical methods, without the prior written permission of the publisher, except in the case of brief quotations embodied in critical reviews and certain other noncommercial uses permitted by copyright law. For permission requests, write to the publisher, addressed "Attention: Book Rights and Permission," at the address below.

Published in the United States of America

ISBN 978-1-960684-49-3 (SC)
ISBN 978-1-960684-47-9 (HC)
ISBN 978-1-960684-48-6 (Ebook)

J and G Publication
222 West 6th Street
Suite 400, San Pedro, CA, 90731
www.stellarliterary.com

Order Information and Rights Permission:

Quantity sales. Special discounts might be available on quantity purchases by corporations, associations, and others. For details, contact the publisher at the address above.

For Book Rights Adaptation and other Rights Permission. Call us at toll-free 1-888-945-8513 or send us an email at admin@stellarliterary.com.

I would like to dedicate
Believe, Believe, Believe
to my wife, Gwen.

I see your continual growth, and I know that
you are experiencing victories in your life,
because you
Believe, Believe, Believe the Word of God.

I love you, Gwen, and I
am proud of you.
Keep pressing.

...this book will cause you to believe the word of God like you have never believed it before!

Lincoln's Believe, Believe, Believe possesses a clear, sermon-like quality, which is appropriate, since the book is written for Christians and others interested in the Christian faith. Using quotes from the Bible, analogies, definitions from the dictionary, and real-life experiences, the text moves along intensely, dispensing a code of conduct based on obedience to God and the Word of God. As Lincoln states at the end of his introduction, "I pray this book will cause you to believe the word of God like you have never believed it before."

Overall, Lincoln's premise is fairly simple: Everyone should believe God, and not man. Lincoln believes that if readers take the initial first step, everything else in their lives will come together in a good way. In making this point, Lincoln covers nearly every aspect of Christianity: belief—what to believe, what not to believe, belief in Jesus Christ, the blessed and the cursed, and other distinctly Christian ideals.

The most interesting discussions in Believe, Believe, Believe are Lincoln's attacks upon the devil. Lincoln describes him as, among other things, a phony, a liar, and a bringer of division. In nearly every chapter, Lincoln takes time to confront the devil. "Both Christians and non-Christians blame God for accidents, deaths, and other tragic things in life," Lincoln writes. "Was it God or was it the devil? Most people know the answer—the devil." Such a clever call and response technique is commonplace in Christianity, and Lincoln is quite effective and entertaining when he makes good use of it. Lincoln calls for unconditional commitment to the Christian faith. Believe, Believe, Believe is a fine book.

Believe, Believe, Believe

The Victory Is In Your Heart

Introduction

Many Christians do not trust God completely to meet their every need. Their belief in God is limited. Some believe God can heal them, but they can't believe that He could prosper them or change their wayward child.

And Jesus, replying, said to them, "Have faith in God (constantly). Truly I tell you, whoever says to this mountain, 'Be lifted up and thrown into the sea,' and does not doubt at all in his heart but believes that what he says will take place, it will be done for him. For this reason I am telling you, whatever you ask for in prayer, believe (trust and be confident) that it is granted to you, and you will (get it)" (Mark 11:22–24).

If you have constant faith in God, and do not doubt at all, you shall have whatever you ask in the will of God. Believing God and God's Word will get you God's promises. No mountain in life can stand in the way of the God-kind of faith. From Jesus' own lips, we receive the most direct and practical instruction concerning our faith:

(a) that our faith be "in God," our living Father, and in agreement with His will and Word; and
(b) that we "believe," not doubting in our hearts.

Thus, "speaking" to the mountain is not a vain exercise of the lips, but an applied release of God's creative words of promise to move in the situation. God spoke the world into existence because He believed it would happen. We can speak our world into existence by the Word of God, if we Believe, Believe, Believe it can happen.

Believing can only work for you when you have faith in what God's word says. When you believe that God exists and that He loves you and wants to meet your needs, your believing becomes action. In other words, you act on what you believe. When you believe that God exists and loves you, but you don't think He will meet your needs—maybe someone else's needs, but not yours—you are in doubt, or unbelief. I pray this book will cause you to believe the Word of God like you have never believed it before.

Chapter One

Why Believe?

...If you acknowledge and confess with your lips that Jesus is Lord and in your heart believe (adheres to, trust in, and rely on the truth) that God raised Him from the dead, you will be saved. For with the heart a person believes (adhere to, trust in, and relies on Christ) and so is justified (declared righteous, acceptable to God), and with the mouth he confesses (declares openly and speaks out freely his faith) and confirms (his) salvation (Rom. 10:9–10).

Believing corrects our relationship with God. By believing and confessing, you will be saved. You position yourself to be declared the righteous of God, and also acceptable to God. Believing also confirms your own salvation in Christ.

Why believe? To position yourself in the Body of Christ and the Family of God. When you believe, you open up the arms of God to receive your spirit, soul, and body. Believing positions you to start hearing from your Heavenly Father on a daily basis.

Why believe? You position yourself to receive the blessings of Abraham upon your life, and also the lives of your loved ones.

Why believe? It takes you out of the kingdom of darkness and plants you in the Kingdom of God. Believing starts you on the road to righteousness. Believing will help you arrive at a recognition and knowledge of the truth.

These weak women will listen to anybody who will teach them; they are forever inquiring and getting information, but never able to arrive at a recognition and knowledge of the truth (2 Tim. 3:7).

Why believe? You will recognize that you have been going the wrong way for years. Everyone wants to go the right way in life. Believing will cause you to recognize that abundant life is the right way to go. You will shoot for the higher life in Christ Jesus, and not the lower life in Satan. Believing will cause you to desire God's will in thought, purpose, and action.

Why believe? You are made in the image of God and not in the image of Satan. God is your real Father—Satan is a phony. Why believe? With believing comes victory in every area of your life.

Why believe? So you may be proficient, and thoroughly equipped for every good work.

Why believe? Because God's Word is alive and full of power that brings eternal blessings to you.

Why believe? You would be a fool not to believe the Word of God. Think about this: Think of any person who is born again. What changed that person? Who changed that person? I know you are saying I know the answer, but do you truly know?

This book is about believing, believing, believing. If we asked two people those questions, you would get two different answers, but each of us who is born again experienced the same surgery of the heart.

Why believe? When you believe what the Word of God says—you are set free. Freedom is another reason to believe the Word of God. What are you free from? Free from the deception of the devil. Free from the lies of the devil. Free from sickness and disease attacking your body. When you believe, you are free to call and bring your blessings from the spiritual realm into the natural realm. You achieve the freedom to be a superstar in God's class. Can you see why the devil wants you not to believe? He is exposed when you choose to believe the Word of God. All the promises of God are at your fingertips when you choose to Believe, Believe, Believe.

Why believe? So that God can start showing you the reality of His Word in ways you have never seen before. Get the picture—why does the devil want to keep you in unbelief? Doubt and do without, but believe and receive the freedom to help others experience the blessings of God. You will be free to have two unchangeable things of God: His promise and His oath! You will be free to lean your entire human personality on God in absolute trust and confidence in His power.

Why believe? We are then free to enter into His presence like we never have been before—free to have fellowship with the Almighty God at all times. I hope you Believe, Believe, Believe, the Word of God. For the Word will set you free—whom the Son sets free are free indeed (John 8:36). Free to know the truth, and nothing but the truth, of the gospel of the Lord Jesus Christ. Free to help others find the Way, the Truth, and the Life, who is Jesus Himself.

But when they believed the good news (the gospel) about the kingdom of God and the name of Jesus Christ (the Messiah) as Philip preached it, they were baptized, both men and women. Even Simon himself believed (he adhered to, trusted in, and relied on the teaching of Philip), and after being baptized, devoted himself constantly to him. And seeing signs and miracles of great power which were being performed, he was utterly amazed (Acts 8:12–13).

Believing the Word of God causes you to not only see great power, but also experience greater power in your life. Believing will cause you to devote your life to the gospel of the Lord Jesus Christ. I want to bring to your attention this great power. What is this great power?

How God anointed and consecrated Jesus of Nazareth with the (Holy) Spirit and with strength and ability and power; how He went about doing good and, in particular, curing all who were harassed and oppressed by (the power of) the devil, for God was with Him (Acts 10:38).

This great power is the Holy Spirit. The devil is a liar. He doesn't have power over believers, because we are not his children. We belong to God! Why believe? Because the great power of the Holy Spirit is available to you. The reason the devil fights so hard to keep you from receiving the

Holy Spirit is because the great power that defeated him, and will help you defeat him, is the Holy Spirit. Every born-again believer should receive and be filled with the Holy Spirit. Jesus Himself told the disciples not to move until they received the Holy Spirit. Consider this: Mary, the mother of Jesus, was in that first group of onehundred-and-twenty people who received the Holy Spirit. Peter went from a weak brother to a mighty warrior after receiving the infilling of the Holy Spirit. Can you see why the devil has tricked the Body of Christ for so long, concerning the infilling of the Holy Spirit? A house divided has no power. Catch this, saints (the set apart ones): We have been fooled, but will be fooled no longer.

Why believe? Because great power awaits us to defeat the devil each and every day. Study! Why believe? To be set free by the Word of God. Why believe? So you will know that you are the calledout ones, which is the definition of the Church. We must know who we are in Christ Jesus. Who are Christians? The official definition is believers in Jesus Christ, not unbelievers. To believe you must believe all the truth—not half or three-quarters, but all the truth. God is good, and all He does is good. Why believe? Jesus is coming back soon for his Church—the calledout ones—and if you are in unbelief, you can't go with Him. If you are in unbelief, you are an unbeliever in Jesus Christ—a non-Christian. The Church, or called-out ones, are believers in Jesus Christ, the Body of Christ, Christians. Jesus is only returning for His Body.

Why believe? Only believers will return to Heaven with Jesus. Do you want the wrath of God to fall on you? Think about this question.

Believe what the Word of God says to you. God gave you a choice. Believing brings victory, power, promises, and transportation home to Heaven for the called-out ones. That is why you should believe the Word of God.

Chapter Two

What Are You Believing?

May the God of your hope so fill you with all joy and peace in believing (through the experience of your faith) that by the power of the Holy Spirit you may abound and be overflowing (bubbling over) with hope (Rom. 15:13)

You can see from this verse that believing what the Word of God says will bring you all joy, all peace, and all hope. So what do you believe? Do you believe the lies of the devil, or do you believe the truth of the Word? God says if you are believing, He will give you all joy. That means you will be filled with joy in any situation. Do you believe for all joy? We have a part in this—it is not all God. What is our responsibility? Simply that we must believe the Word of God. It sounds easy, but many unbelieving people say they believe in the Word of God. An example of this can be found in the subject of speaking in tongues. Some believe in speaking in tongues and some do not. Acts 2:4 says, And they were all filled (diffused throughout their souls) with the Holy Spirit and began to speak in other (different, foreign) languages (tongues) as The Spirit kept giving them clear and loud expression (in each tongue in appropriate words).

If you go up to Acts 2:1, you will see that they were the New Testament Church, which began with120 people. Do you believe that tongues are for us today, or not? Sisters and brothers, let me present you one truth, the Church (the called out-ones) began on that day of Pentecost and have never stopped. One of the manifestations of the power of the Holy Spirit is tongues. God gave us tongues for a reason. Come on over to Jude 20:

But you, beloved, build yourselves up (founded) on your most holy faith (make progress, wise like and edifice higher and higher), praying in the Holy Spirit (Jude 20).

Tongues is praying in the Holy Spirit, which builds you up and helps you progress in your Christian walk. Earlier, I said we have unbelievers in the Body of Christ. Tongues is a sign not to the believers, but to the unbelievers. Will you believe what the Word of God says or what someone says? If you can find one man or woman who speaks in tongues, you can believe, because of the Word of God that tongues is for the Church today. God is not a respecter of persons (Acts 10:34).

Believe, Believe, and Believe! Believing brings peace in your life. Jesus said, I will never leave you nor forsake you (Josh. 1:5). Believing what the Word of God says causes the Spirit of Peace to overtake you in every situation in your life. Don't pick and choose what you are going to believe— believe what the Word says completely. Let's believe the Bible. You can break the Bible down like this: it is the best instruction manual that we can have.

We are the Body of Christ. We are not Baptists, Lutherans, or Pentecostals, but Believers. Believers who believe that the Word of God is true, and that Jesus Christ is the Son of God. Also, we believe that He came to die in our place so we would not have to. God is not a God of denominations. People started denominations. God says we are the Body of Christ—period. Not the body of Baptist, or the body of any other denomination. God says there is one Body, and only one Body—not bodies of denominations.

Wake up! Division is of the devil. We are not separate, but one, with One God and one mediator between God and man—and that is the man, Jesus Christ. Either you are a believer in Jesus Christ and the Word of God, or you are an unbeliever. Being an unbeliever will bring death into your life, but to believe will bring abundant life to you. What you believe determines your destiny. Death for the unbeliever, and life for the believer—what are you going to believe? The Word of God, or man?

God's ways and thoughts are higher than our ways and thoughts. Check yourself! What are you believing? At this very moment, are you believing what God's Word says about your situation, or what tradition says about your situation? I call this a truth-check. You can pass or fail. If you pass, the Word of God becomes real to you, and guess what else? Jesus becomes real to you, and abundant life is produced in your life. If you fail by not believing the Word of God, Jesus doesn't become real to you and death is produced in your life.

Believing what the Word of God says will bring abundant blessings of the gospel of Christ into your life. The Spirit of Truth, the Holy Spirit, will help you know the truth which will set you free, if you will allow Him. Your will is involved, you must allow Holy Spirit to reveal the truth to you. He will not force the truth upon you. By inviting the Holy Spirit to do a truth-check on you, you will find out if what you are believing lines up with the Word of God. If what you are believing does not line up with the Word of God, then you need to change.

Faith is an action word. The Word says believe, and you shall receive. The word believe (trust, adhere to, rely on) occurs 98 times throughout the Gospel of John. The assured result of this belief, or faith in Jesus Christ is the possession of eternal life. There are promises for each child of God, if they believe the right thing. God said He would rebuke the devourer if you tithe. That is a promise, but if you don't believe in tithing, He can't rebuke the devourer on your behalf. If you believe tithing is just an Old Testament quirk, then you can't reap the benefits that are yours in the promise. You can't receive a promise if you don't believe that it belongs to you.

Another truth-check! Does the Word of God require us to tithe? What do you believe? Check the Word and the Holy Spirit for the correct answer. All our money belongs to God, but what percent is for the tithe? The Word of God and the Holy Spirit only give the correct answers to you. The textbook is the Bible, and the Author is the Holy Spirit. If you do a truth-check using these guidelines of the Holy Spirit, only then can the Word become important in your life. He, The Spirit of Truth, will keep you in position for a blessing.

Call to Me and I will answer you and show you great and mighty things, fenced in and hidden which you do not know (do not distinguish and recognize, have knowledge of and understand) (Jer. 33:3).

Believing the Word of God will bring mighty, fenced, and hidden things to the surface in your life. To recognize, distinguish, have knowledge, and understand life, you must believe what the Word of God says. Believing is the key to a great and mighty future. When you call on God, be smart enough to recognize that His answer can come through His Word.

What you believe for is what you will receive. If I do not believe that Jesus bore all my sickness, then I will not receive it. My confession is that Jesus bore every sickness—therefore, I don't have to receive sickness. What I believe lines up with the Word of God. If the Word says by Jesus' stripes we are healed, then that is what it means.

Believe, and let the Word of God operate in your life. Many believers are not letting the Word of God operate in their lives. Every Sunday they go to church, but still walk in defeat. Why? I'll tell you why. They simply don't believe the Word of God. Jesus defeated the devil and the devil doesn't have any rule over a believer. That is a true statement, but not a statement of reality in many confessing believers' lives.

We believe more of what the devil says than what the Word of God says. The Word calls us blessed, but if you ask most believers how they are doing—the answer you will get most of the time is, "I am fine." My question is, "What is fine?" Jesus said we are blessed. He is our Head and we are His Body. This being so, we should be saying what the Head is saying about the Body. But many believers don't know what the Word says. When you know what the Word says, you must believe what the Word says. What do you believe? God Himself took the time to get into our hands the handbook of life. The Bible is the only handbook that gives you instructions on how your spirit, soul, and body are to function. Brothers and sisters, it is a must for you to believe what the Word of God says. The organization of the Bible will show you that it was supernaturally put together. Pick any subject and God will give you the truth about it. The news media produces the product of the the devil; the Bible produces the product of the Holy One of Israel. Do you believe that healings are for you today? If sickness has invaded your body and you are in right standing with God, I dare you to believe what the Word of God says, that by His stripes you are healed. Believe what the Word of God says, and all the promises of God will be yours. All the promises of God must be obtained through your believing.

Another word for believing is faith. God says that without faith, it is impossible to please Him. Another way of saying that is, without believing, it is impossible to please God. Catch this truth: If you are in disbelief, you are not pleasing God. God's Word is forever settled in Heaven—and also, God is not a man that He should tell or act a lie (Num. 23:19). God's Word is settled. What does that mean? God's Word never changes. If we have any challenges, then we must check ourselves. Catch this truth: No sickness or disease can stay in the body of a believer, because Jesus has already borne every sickness and disease in His body. If it is in His Body, it can't be in your body. I dare you to believe that it is in His body. If you can believe that it is in His body, it can't be in your body. If it is in His body, it left your body. I dare you to believe the Word of God!

You may be saying, Brother, I know people who are sick and call themselves believers. The Word of God can't lie! Some situation is causing the condition of a lie to be in the believer's life. Ignorance is a condition. Most of the time, it is the condition that is keeping the believer sick. Ignorance to the Word of God is a condition that will keep a believer sick. When truth enters into a believer's life, sickness must go.

We must not be ignorant of the devil's tactics any longer. We are more than conquerors and world overcomers in Christ Jesus (Rom. 8:37). Do you believe the lies of the devil? This book is a wake-up call for the Body of Christ. It is meant for every member of the Body—not just pastors, and teachers, but everyone.

Brothers and sisters, go back and check out the history of the Church. The book of Acts is a good place to start. I challenge your belief: What do you believe, the Word of God, or tradition and the devil? Believing and receiving the Word of God will cause you to soar like an eagle—God made us to soar high above the ground of life. What we believe causes us either to soar above the ground of life, or crash to the ground of life. We are in charge of how high we go in life, or how low we go in life. We can choose to believe and receive, and go high in life, or we can choose to doubt and do without, and go low in life. This is also a book about choices. I hope you make the right choice in life! The Bible says that the eagle is keen in vision. We believers are to be as keen in vision as the eagle. We are never to take our eyes off of Jesus. This can be only accomplished by believing what is right and doing what is right.

We must watch with whom we hang around. Some of the most spiritual people get off track (Jim Jones, for example). Take a watchful look to see if you are in the land of eagles, or the land of chickens. If you are in the land of the chickens, your belief status needs checking. Your mind has been fenced in by unbelief. Only the shining of the Word of God on your mind can tighten belief in the Word of God. Your mind has been taken captive by unbelief from the devil.

Again, what do you believe—the Word of God, or tradition and the devil? The Word of God is to be believed above anything else. It is the Word of Truth!

Chapter Three

Who Are You Believing?

Who do you believe? You may say, "I know whom I am believing." That could be true. In this world, three voices speak to you. First, the voice of the Lord; second, the voice of the flesh; and third, the voice of the devil. Do you really know who is speaking to you?

At any given time, one or another can speak to you. The one who has most of your attention is the one you hear the most. Let's get something settled: if you are not spending time with the Lord, you will not recognize His voice. Which voice has most of your attention—the Lord's, the flesh's, or the devil's? If it is the voice of the Lord, He will tell you things that line up with the Word of God. The voice of the flesh will tell you things that line up with pleasing you. The voice of the devil will tell you things that line up with the pleasures of this world.

You should not be confused about who is speaking to you at any given time. The voice of the Lord will guide you by the Word of God! That is one of the ways you can know if you are hearing from God. Go to the Word of God. If what you are being told does not line up with the Word of God, tune it out.

An example of what to believe: the Word says not to judge others— to love all people. You are to believe the best of all people. Don't judge them! Because all people are made in the image of God, you should not hate anyone. Someone may not know he or she was made in the image of God, but it is not up for debate. Don't get confused—a person does not have to operate in the image of God. The reality remains: all are made in the image of God. Inside of each person, the likeness of God waits to be born. Once we are born again, we understand that we have the image of God there all the time inside of us. You might say, "I do not believe that." That is ok! The Word of God says, God said, "Let Us (Father, Son, and Holy Spirit) make mankind in Our image, after Our likeness, and let them have complete authority over the fish of the sea, the birds of the air, the beasts, and over all of the earth, and over everything that creeps upon the earth" (Gen. 1:26).

What are you going to believe? You might say, "I do not like that person." Whose voice are you listening to? The thought did not just appear. The voice you hear, which sounded like yours, was in reality the voice of the flesh or the devil. How do I know that? Because God so loved the world that He gave His Only-begotten Son (John 3:16). God is Love! He is not hate.

Who do you believe? If you allow the Lord to control you, He does the best job you could imagine: But He needs your consent. The flesh and the devil do not ask for your consent, they act without your permission. The flesh and the devil are takers—God is a giver. Look around any major city and you will see people living on the streets. Have you ever asked yourself why these people are on the streets? It is not because of a lack of education.

Let me take you on a trip down spiritual lane. The voice most of these people have heard all their lives—which they thought was their own, and in reality it was not—belonged to the flesh or the devil. You ask me how I know that. Who in their right mind would want to live on the streets? God provided mankind with a home from day one. What person would want to live like these people are living? You can't find one person.

I know you are thinking "most of these people can't help the circumstances in life." Yes, they can! If they start believing the Most High God (El Elyon) loves them and they turn to Him, then everything will turn for them. I can prove what I have just written. In the Book of Instructions Before Leaving Earth, which you might recognize as the Holy Bible, there is an outline:

If my people, who are called by My name, shall humble themselves, pray, seek, crave, and require of necessity My face and turn from their wicked ways, then will I hear from Heaven, forgive their sin, and heal their land (2 Chron. 7:14).

God has set us up! If we do something, He will do something. Those people living on the streets across America do not have to continue in such circumstances. If the instruction outlined in 2 Chronicles 7:14 is followed, these circumstances must depart. You do not have to be born again to call out to God. He is the Creator of mankind! The requirement is to humble yourself, pray, seek, crave, and require of necessity God's face. Every person on the face of the earth can do that.

The Love of God says you do not have to live the way you are living, but if you will not believe or read the Word of God, you will never have all that God wants you to have. Life is not as hard as mankind has made it out to be. God, in His wisdom, has laid out the game plan.

If we refuse to follow the game plan drawn up by God, we can't win the game of life. We look at the Bible as a strange book—yet, it is the Book through which God speaks to us. The Bible is God's game plan for every life that comes on earth.

It is very simple! When you start playing baseball or football, you start in peewee league and work your way up, until one day you reach the Pros. If you are blessed enough to get to the Pros on your ability, but then run the wrong plays, you risk causing defeat to the team and serious injury to yourself. If you run the wrong plays in life, you face defeat by the devil, and worse, the game of eternity is passing you by.

Can you understand the purpose in believing what the Word of God has to say? Do not let the most important voice (the Lord's) go unheard. God is still speaking today, but most people do not know the voice of God. If we take the time to pray, seek, and crave God, we will then know whom we are believing. You will know when the voice of God is speaking, and when it is the voice of the flesh, or the voice of the devil speaking. People say all the time, "I am waiting on God to tell me what to do." God is waiting on you to tell Him what you are going to do. The Word of God says, Call to Me and I will answer you and show you great and mighty things, fenced in and hidden, which you do not know (do not distinguish and recognize, have knowledge of and understand) (Jer. 33:3).

Each person born into this earth has a purpose and plan from God. The only way you are going to find out your purpose is to call to God. Things that are fenced in and hidden from you are waiting to be found. God has the perfect mate for you, and if you do not call to Him, you will marry the first person who comes along. We are in a battle! One side is good (God's) and one side is evil (Satan's). Each one of us starts the battle on the side of evil, because of the fall of Adam. But, because of the resurrection of Jesus, we do not need to remain on the evil side.

God promises that if we will call to Him, He will show us things we do not have knowledge of, or understand. You can't beat the goodness of God! The Commander-In-Chief of the good side is God, and He plans on blessing His soldiers for a job well done. The Commander-In-Chief of the evil side is Satan, and he plans on cursing his soldiers for a job well done. Whose side will you be on?

Myself, I have chosen the good side. The devil does not have any new tricks. Deception is deception! He deceived Adam and Eve, and he has been deceiving the world ever since. A thought for the day: If you have been believing what the flesh and the devil have been telling you—deception has taken place. The good side is home to blessings and truth. Curses and lies are on the evil side.

The choice is yours. Who are you willing to believe? One thing I know for sure is that the Lord is good and He will bless his people. Evidence has been presented to the jury that God is in the blessing business. Are you going to believe the voice of the flesh and the voice of the devil, or are you going to believe the voice of the Lord? The voice of the flesh and the voice of the devil will take you away from the blessings of God, but the voice of the Lord will take you toward the blessings of God.

Believe this—God is always trying to give something to you! He never tries to take anything away. God has gotten a bad reputation. Believing God will get unseen things into your life. Stop! Be still. Let the Love of God overtake you and place you right in the middle of the will of God for your life. He will reveal the plan and purpose for you being here on earth. He will give you the script, and His angels are assigned to make sure you get safely from the field of life to the field of greatness. When you listen to the voice of the Lord—greatness pays you a visit!

Greatness wants to take you from the outhouse to the White House. Greatness wants to take you from common labor and make you the president of the company. You can only hear greatness when the voice of the Lord is speaking. You cannot hear greatness when the voice of the flesh or the voice of the devil is speaking. You might say, "I know many great men or women in the United States that do not listen to the voice of the Lord." Yes, by the standards of the world, that is a correct statement —but in the eyes of the Lord, that is a false statement. Greatness can only come when you submit yourself to the will of God, and let Him mold you into the person He wants you to be.

Jesus was asked a question by His disciples on greatness. He answered by saying that whoever wants to be great in the Kingdom of God must first be willing to be a servant to others. Serving others is rewarding and fulfilling. When you hear and obey the voice of the Lord, goodness and mercy show up in your life. Goodness and mercy will follow you all the days of your life (Ps. 23:6). They camp out in your life to make sure your life is rewarding. You can only hear goodness and mercy through the voice of the Lord—they cannot be heard through the voice of the flesh or the voice of the devil.

I have some good news. Goodness and mercy are looking for you, with a special blessing from the Lord. That is something to shout about! I can't tell you what that blessing is, but what I can tell you is God is a good God. Whether a small or large blessing, it is a blessing with your name on it. If you are able to read this book, that is a blessing. If you are able to walk to the bank, that is a blessing: Some folks can do neither. If you are able to drive a car or van, that is a blessing. If you have a job to go to, that is a blessing.

Everything we have has been given to us by God! God is still in control. If you choose to listen to the voice of the flesh or the voice of the devil, God will allow you to do so. You might say, "that does not sound right." Regardless, God did not, and will not, take away man's right to choose. Whatever you choose in your life, He will allow you to do it. In that sense, God is like any parent: you are free to choose; He will not force you to make the choice He desires. You might not be where God wants you, but He will not make you grow. The growth in your relationship with God comes from believing, and receiving from God. You will not grow in your relationship with God believing what the voice of the flesh and the voice of the devil are saying.

Are you at the level of your Christian life where God wants you to be? If you are not, you can start today by reading the Word of God more, praying more, and fasting more. Praying and fasting will cause you to hear the voice of the Lord clearly. Increase your fasting and praying, and see God's plan for your life unfold before your eyes.

You might say, "I can't tell the voice of God from the voice of the flesh, or the voice of the devil." I want to tackle a religious tradition: God does not speak to your mind—God speaks to your spirit! I will back up what I say with the Word of God.

Let's look at the Scriptures. Romans 8:16—The Spirit Himself (thus) testifies together with our own spirit, (assuring us) that we are children of God.

Who is the "Spirit Himself?" He is the Holy Spirit, and the Holy Spirit is God! The Holy Spirit will give you an inner witness of something, and that is God speaking to your spirit—not to your mind. God is a Spirit! God speaks directly to your spirit-man—the real you— and you, in your mind, get the urgency to do or say something. But God does not speak directly to your mind. The thoughts that come to your mind must line up with the Word of God and also with the plan for your life.

You say, God told me to go to South Carolina to start a church. When you get to South Carolina, everything should be in place, because God is a provider. If things are not, then the flesh or the devil spoke to you. God will not leave you hanging! Our Pastor was told to start a ministry 20 years ago. Did he hear from God? In the beginning, he prayed and fasted for three days to make sure it was God telling him to start a ministry and not the flesh or the devil. He started with 17 people, and the ministry now includes over 8,000 members and is known nationwide.

Did he hear from God? The evidence in front of us concludes he did. The devil would not have let this ministry go on for 20 years, helping others to be set free from bondage. The devil is not in the business of bringing glory to God. Remember Jim Jones—how many people died in Jim Jones' ministry?

God adds; The devil subtracts. The Word of God says, "the devil came to steal, kill, and destroy." Those who had attached themselves to Jim Jones had their dreams killed and destroyed, along with their physical selves. We can say the same thing about the destruction of the Branch Davidians, in Waco, Texas.

Another instruction in the Word of God may help you: Romans 8:14— For all who are led by the Spirit of God are the sons of God. If the Spirit of God leads you, then you will know what is false and what is true, because the Spirit of God is the Spirit of Truth. The Spirit of Truth leads you into all truth. The two incidents mentioned above show why it is important to know the voice of the Lord. In each incident, death was the final reward.

The devil is not playing—he knows his time is very short. Why would you be playing, then? He is out to take as many people as he can to Hell with him. Wake up! The devil is throwing a party for all those who want to join him in the lake of fire. God, on the other hand, is trying with all His heart to let us know the plans of the devil.

If you heard a man of God (preacher) but have not listened to him, I beseech you, please listen! We are in the last days, and time is running out. Every true man of God is pouring out the revelation of the Word God has given him in the last days to save your soul from destruction. I am not trying to scare anyone, but reality is reality. The Word of God is your shield and buckler. It will keep you safe. It will put supernatural abundance into your life. It will make the enemy your footstool. It will cause your loved ones to change. It will make your marriage a happy union. It will keep sickness and disease away from you. It will bring wealth into your hands, for you to be a blessing in the Body of Christ. It will bring you before great men. It will cause you to be the lender and not the borrower. It will cause you to be the head and not the tail. It will take weak persons and make them into strong persons.

Seek God with all your heart! You must give yourself wholeheartedly to God. I said I wasn't trying to scare you, but I have changed my mind. Yes, I am trying to scare you! I want you to fight for what has been promised to you and what is already yours in the Body of Christ. If you are born again, you are in the Army of God, and all these things belong to you. Hear me! Satan does not like you, and is out to kill, steal, and destroy you. It is time for you to wake up. Satan is the deceiver of mankind! He does not like you any more than he likes God.

The war (spiritual war) is still going on. It is the longest war on earth (over 2,000 years). We have a Supernatural Commander-In-Chief (God Almighty), but many in the Body of Christ are POWs. Our Commander-In-Chief is waiting to accomplish anything and all things for His troops. The Word of God says, You do not have, because you do not ask (Jas. 4:2). Many of the troops do not ask because they do not spend time in prayer and do not know the voice of the Lord.

All people recognize their earthly father's voice, but do not recognize their Heavenly Father's voice. Who are you believing? Where is your spirit? It is your conscience.

The Vine's Expository Dictionary says the conscience is that faculty by which we apprehend the will of God, as that which is designed to govern our lives, hence (a) the sense of guiltiness before God; (b) that process of thought which distinguishes what it considers morally good or bad, condemning the good, condemning the bad, and so prompting to do the former, and avoid the latter.

Each person has a conscience. When you become a believer, your conscience—which was against God—is now able to hear the voice of the Lord. If you are a believer, you know what is morally right and what is morally wrong. It comes down to what you do with the information after it is processed in your conscience. If the Holy Spirit controls you, you will by the apprehension of God's presence, realize that griefs are to be borne in accordance with His will. This will happen if you are or are not controlled by the Holy Spirit. Wrong actions bring grief into your conscience.

For you to know the will of God, God has provided His Holy Spirit, but you must recognize the prompting of the Holy Spirit in your conscience. God is a good God. He never intended for mankind to experience any bad. Adam's conscience was morally good until he ate of the tree of the knowledge of good and evil. Once Adam sinned against God, his eyes were opened to morally good and morally bad. He saw his, as well as Eve's nakedness as morally bad.

In the Vines, knowledge is defined as to fully perceive, or notice attentively. Do you understand why God did not want Adam and Eve to eat of the tree of the knowledge of good and evil? Once they did, they began to perceive morally good and morally evil. They did not know of evil prior to their eating from the tree.

In this world, things are called wrong which are right, and called right which are wrong. God is morally good! How can He have fellowship with His children, if sometimes they are morally good and sometimes they are morally bad? It could not happen! That is why Jesus came to earth: to destroy the works of the evil one.

The devil (morally bad) introduced Adam and Eve to his nature. There is only one bloodline, and it came from Adam and Eve, who are the first parents. It's been proven that all of mankind—every race, all cultures—have the same bloodline. When our first parents committed high treason, good and bad were allowed to co-exist on earth—but prior to the fall of mankind, only good existed. The Word of God says that everything He made was not only good, but very good. God can't be in the presence of bad; for that reason, He kicked Adam and Eve out of the Garden of Eden. All was well until they let evil become part of their nature.

God is in control and Satan wants to be in control. God allows the devil to test us. It is up to each one of us to prove him (the devil) wrong and God right. Will you let the Holy Spirit lead you, so you can hear the voice of the Lord? You do not have to settle for the natural (lower) life—all the supernatural (higher) life is waiting for you. Fellowship with God, so you can know the voice of the Lord and respond to Him in a loving and caring manner.

I ask you to purpose in your heart to allow the Holy Spirit to have free course in your life. It is a new day! Allow the Almighty God to have complete control of your life—you will never, ever be the same again.

Chapter Four

What Not to Believe

What we believe or do not believe affects every area of our lives. Not one area of your life goes untouched—not one. What you believe or do not believe will have an impact on you as a whole person. For example, those told as children that they wouldn't amount to much almost always unknowingly set out to make this false statement true. The false statement—"you won't amount to much"—is something you wouldn't want to believe on your life. Do you know who is behind this lie? The devil is the one hiding behind this lie.

God has made us in His image. Every human being is capable of being the best person on earth, because we have been made in God's image. What does the Bible mean by image? The Bible says we are made in the image of God, but you must ask yourself this question—what is image? One of the definitions of image is an exact likeness. We are to be exactly like God on the inside. What is on the inside of us will produce what is going on around us. So you say, "that is not true—I cannot be producing the things that are going on around me." Well, what are you choosing to believe, or not to believe?

Some examples of what not to believe: my wife does not love me, because she chose to sleep tonight instead of having sex, or, my husband does not love me, because he chose to sleep tonight instead of having sex. Your wife or husband could have had a rough day at work. Their love for you has nothing to do with them not wanting to have sex.

Inside of you is the correct image. If love is inside of us, we will think the best of each person. We will not think that our wives or husbands do not love us just because they do not want to have sex. If you choose not to believe that we are made in the image of God, you will produce from the inside those images attributed to the devil and not to God.

Lying comes from the devil. The Bible says the devil is the father of lies. There is no truth in him. Then, why on earth do we continue to believe him? The Bible says, Wine is a mocker. Strong drink is a brawler. And whoever is led astray by it is not wise (Prov. 20:1).

This is the Bible, not my own opinion. I am just repeating what the Bible says. Why do we continue to drink, and think we are having fun? The person led astray by wine or strong drink is not wise—if you are not wise, then you are unwise. Another word for unwise is to be a fool.

In our town, we have a new baseball team. I recently took my son to a game, and so many people were drinking beer as if it was water. It is a brawler—beer came to brawl against you. Another lie from the devil: beer is good. Something, or someone assigned to brawl against you is not fun or good.

Can you see how this lie is destroying many people? They start with wine, and move to beer, and then to stronger drinks. Each step increases their ability to brawl with themselves. They get out of control, and are controlled by what they drink. The truth is that they have allowed something to control their life other than God. The reality is that beer or strong drink becomes their God instead of the living God, who has all you want or need.

One verse in the Bible says that the Spirit of Truth will teach you all things (John 14:26). The Spirit of Truth is the Holy Spirit, or Spirit of God—God Himself! Don't believe the devil, who came to kill, steal, and destroy you in every area of your life.

Look around any city in the United States of America, and you will see evidence of his stealing from and destroying the lives of Americans. Homeless people believe they are homeless and that there is nowhere for them to live, but if they just came to Jesus and surrendered, He would provide for all their needs. Jesus gave us life—and not just life, but abundant life.

Jesus said He would not leave us or forsake us (John 14:18). If you choose not to believe that Jesus came to give you abundant life, you will never receive abundant life. You have settled for the lies of the devil and authorized him to operate in your life. The devil takes advantage of your weakness. Most people know the story of Eve. The devil took advantage of her weakness, and similarly, he will take advantage of your weakness. If you do not want him in your life, then choose for him not to operate in your life and do not believe his lies. You can say I do not believe that. Well, let's go to the Bible again. The Bible says, Death and life are in the power of the tongue (Prov. 18:21).

A person's life largely reflects the fruit of his tongue. To speak life is to speak God's perspective on any issue of life; to speak death is to declare life's negatives, to declare defeat, or complain constantly.

Would Jesus still help a homeless person who came to Him without surrendering his or her heart to Him? This question has been answered many times. Jesus can and will help that individual to a point—but the amount of help may be hindered if the homeless person has not surrendered his or her heart to Jesus.

Have you seen people who seem to never get it together in life? Most likely, they have not surrendered their hearts to Jesus. Jesus is the doorway to the Father God. His whole Body must be allowed to come into your heart. Those who will not allow Jesus to enter into their hearts face great danger. They believe they can take care of life's situations on their own. This is an example of what not to believe.

We were not made to carry the load. Put on your thinking cap and think about this next sentence: Adam was not weaned from God, he choose to wean himself, by listening to Eve, who had listened to the devil! Adam had all the physical tools, but not the spiritual tools to survive. When God put Adam out of the Garden of Eden, Adam had not been weaned, he didn't have all the spiritual tools to combat whatever the devil threw at him. He could have lived another 900 or so years physically, but not spiritually.

Most people have never let God wean them. We can only be weaned through intimacy with the Almighty God. We must be equipped with spiritual equipment to war successfully against the devil. God holds the combat equipment in His hand.

Most people think they can make it in this world on their own. Yet the truth is that only complete and unqualified reliance upon the Living Lord will keep you from being swallowed up by this world's systems— and by the devil himself. Surrender is the key that unlocks the vault of God. Choose not to believe, and you will not have God's best and deepest treasures. We have a generation of strong-willed, independent young men and women in whose vocabulary the word surrender does not appear.

Thinking you can cover all the bases yourself will cost you the most important game of your life. Some bases will not be covered because of self-will, and other bases because of independence, and others still because of pride. Even if you get the bases loaded, you will not get a grand slam, because you have not surrendered completely to Jesus. You will leave the bases of life loaded every time.

Surrender is not a popular word, but in order to have God's best for your life, you must depolarize the word and surrender. What not to believe? That free will is the best way to go. Exchanging your will for the will of the One who made Heaven and earth is more of a bargain for you than holding onto your will.

When we exchange our will for God's will, we function in a tangible or visible representation of Him. The visible representation of Him is the image everyone should see in a child of God. That is why it is important for the devil to get you to believe a lie—it takes away from your visible representation of God. Jesus was a visible representation of God the Father when He walked the earth, and we should be too. We, the church (the called-out ones) are to be a visible representation of Christ to the world.

Our image was given to us for us to do something with it. We are a visible representation of the Body of Christ on earth. If you believe that you are not the visible representation of Christ, then you never will be—but if you believe you are the visible representation of Christ, then you will be.

It is so simple—surrender all that you are to the Lord, and watch Him make you all that you can be in the Lord. The return is awesome! Please don't believe that you are just dirt, or that you are nothing. We are dirt only because we came from dirt, but at the same time, we are more than dirt. "I am just dirt" is the wrong belief. We, the children of the Most High God, are more than conquerors, world overcomers.

Confess the Word of God over yourself and your loved ones. Never believe you don't have a purpose for living. God made everyone with a purpose! Your job is to find the purpose for your life. God made all of us with a purpose. What is yours? Don't believe you were an accident. Perhaps your parents may not have planned to have you when you were born, but God planned you long ago, before the foundation of the earth.

God needs people to carry out His plans on earth. Intimacy with the Almighty will cause you to know without a doubt the plan and purpose for your life. What not to believe? That you are just here on earth without a future. What not to believe? The world's words.

What to believe? The Word of God. It will take you, keep you, strengthen you, help you to mature in God. You must believe something in life—why not make it God's Word? Confess God's Word over yourself on a daily basis. It will change your image of yourself to God's image of you.

Chapter Five

Unbelief Destroys Your Rest

Unbelief is the enemy of belief. Belief is the calm assurance and peace in the midst of turmoil, conflict and confusion. Scripture says, Let us labour therefore to enter into that rest, lest any man fall after the same example of unbelief (Heb. 4:11). If you are in unbelief about anything concerning God, then your rest in God is interrupted.

Merriam Webster's Collegiate Dictionary describes rest as a freedom from activity or labor. Think about this description for a moment. If you are in unbelief concerning God's Word, then you are not enjoying freedom from activity or labor. God says He is our shield. If we don't let God be our shield for whatever reason, then all the labor we get into is felt directly by us.

Why do you see Christians and non-Christians experiencing depression? The main reason for this action is unbelief. We can call it anything under the sun, but we were not made to be separated from God. God is the Designer of mankind. We are to believe what the Designer said to do. We got to stay hooked up with God in order to enjoy rest. Unbelief destroys this rest.

I want you to think a moment about this next sentence: you cannot take a Chevy part and put it on a Ford. It does not work like that. We are Godly made! Most people, Christians and NonChristians alike are trying to serve a ungodly god—Satan. It can't be done in the sense that all the good benefits belong to God. He is a just rewarder of those who diligently seek Him. Satan has all the bad benefits, and he too rewards those who diligently seek him.

Stop and think about unbelief. Well now that you have thought about unbelief, let me tell you what Merriam Webster's Collegiate Dictionary says that unbelief is incredulity or skepticism, especially in matters of religious faith.

The Word of God says it is impossible to please God without faith. Can you see why the devil wants everyone in unbelief? Because if you operate in unbelief, then you make your faith void and you do not please God. That makes the devil happy, because He enjoys a person who is not pleasing to God. You are then a vessel that the devil can use. Instead of operating in faith an pleasing God, you are now operating in unbelief and displeasing God.

When you operate in unbelief, you are operating contrary to the Christian character. Another word for unbelief is doubt. You can say that you have a lack of faith in the truth of God's Word. Unbelief is a genuine doubt, based upon suspicions that have been placed in your mind by the devil. The Word of God says:

And do not be conformed to this world, but be transformed by the renewing of your mind, that you may prove what is that good and acceptable and perfect will of God (Rom. 12:2).

Unbelief does not want you to renew your mind. Renew implies a restoration of what had become faded or return to an original state. Unbelief destroys your mind and robs God of His place in your life.

God gives you the blueprint, His Word, which is how you are going to rid yourself of unbelief and doubt. I beseech you, by the mercies of God, to rid yourself of unbelief. The God of Abraham, the God of Jacob, the God of Isaac wants you to make a commitment to Him. When you commit to God your life all the way, nothing hemming and hawing, but saying Jesus, I want to receive all that you done at Calvary and I Thank You for it by allowing you to be Lord over my life, then you are on the road to believing, believing, believing what the Word of God says.

Unbelief robs Jesus of being Lord of your life. Jesus died to give you not only life, but life more abundantly. Unbelief robs Him of the complete right to represent you in the Heavenly court. Do not get me wrong—Jesus is always representing us, but unbelief interrupts His freedom to act on our behalf at the right time.

If you are under attack with a cold and you do not believe that by the stripes of Jesus you can be healed, then at that moment, you stop Jesus from freely acting on your behalf against the opposing attorney— the devil. If only you could see with the spiritual eyes that have been given to you. Every day Jesus is acting on the behalf of one of our brothers or sisters. He is either doing it with the faith you send Him or the unbelief you send Him. Either way, He must stand against our enemy—the devil in the Heavenly court and defend us to the Judge of all judges—God the Heavenly Father.

Believe the Word of God. It is very important that you do. Your spiritual destiny and eternal future hangs on you not operating in unbelief. Unbelief undermines your relationship with God. You can't have a strong relationship with someone you don't trust. Your protection is tied to your belief in God and who He is. The Scriptures tell us:

Now see that I, even I, and there is no God besides Me; I kill and I make alive; I wound and I heal; nor is there any who can deliver from My hand (Deut. 32:39).

Unbelief brings a companion along with it—disloyalty and belief brings a companion along with it —loyalty. God is looking to show Himself strong on the behalf of those who operate in loyalty versus those who operate in disloyalty. To operate in unbelief caused you to be against the maker of Heaven and earth. God is a good God. God is more then enough. He is a shield to those who put their trust in Him.

For the eyes of the Lord run to and fro throughout the whole earth, to show Himself strong on behalf of those whose heart is loyal to Him (2 Chron. 16:9).

Your rest is destroyed if you are worrying about the circumstances of the world. If God is running throughout the earth to show Himself strong—then you can rest assured that all will be well with you.

We have looked at the definition of rest in the Merriam Webster's Dictionary now let's examine the Vine's. Rest in the Vine's is not a "rest" from work, but in work, not the rest of inactivity but the harmonious working of all the faculties and affections—of will, heart, imagination, conscience—because each has found in God the ideal sphere for its satisfaction and development.

Without the maker, who is God, you cannot have what I have described. This rest is not for someone operating in unbelief.

Also in the Vine's unbelief is always rendered disobedience. God honors obedience, He does not honor disobedience. God honors belief, He does not honor unbelief. Disobedience is unwilling to be persuaded. The Word of God, if truly examined will persuade anyone that God is a good God, and He sent His Son into the world not to condemn the world, but that through the Son, the world would be saved.

Many people, Christians, and non-Christians, fall into the category of disobedient. Many Christians are not persuaded of the whole gospel, they accept part, but not the whole gospel as the truth. A godly grandmother who does not operate in the whole gospel can persuade Christians that the gospel is not true, just as much as non-Christians can be persuaded by the world that the gospel is not true. In either case, the spirit of disobedience is in operation.

Your eternal future is at stake. It is very important that you don't operate in the spirit of disobedience. What is one of the caused of unbelief? The answer can be found in Hebrews 3:12. God said that an evil heart is the direct cause of unbelief. You may say, "Well that is fine, but I can't have an evil heart—I have been saved for 15 years." Well you can! If you have never allowed the Holy Spirit of God to examine your heart (soul, mind) then you are operating with the same heart you entered the Kingdom of God with. When you were born again into the Kingdom of God, your spirit was the only thing changed into the image of God. Your soul, body, and mind did not get saved. Your spirit got saved, which is the real you!

Therefore beware brethren, take care, lest there be in any one of you a wicked, unbelieving heart (which refuses to cleave to, trust in, and rely on Him), leading you to turn away and desert or stand aloof from the living God (Heb. 3:12).

Another cause of unbelief is sin. What is sin? One definition in the Vine's for sin is an act of disobedience to divine law. Another definition is missing the mark. God has already established how we are to live by His Word. We miss the mark by not following His instructions, which is sinning against God.

Many people, the church and the unchurched, fall into this category, sinning against God. Many have no clue that all the troubles of their lives are brought on because they are sinning against God. They have missed the mark of His instruction and therefore are living on the instructions of the devil.

Do not be caught in the web of unbelief. It is deadly to be in the web of unbelief. Your eternal destiny depends on you not falling into the trap of unbelief. It has been laid for you over the generations, but hear what the Spirit of God is saying to you.

Arise and sleep no longer. Examine yourself and allow the Holy Spirit to examine you for unbelief. The greatest trap of the devil is unbelief. He is the father of lies—do not believe his lies any longer. How long is eternity? If you think eternity is for just a short while, think again. Eternity is forever, forever, and forever! Can you see now, how important it is to examine yourself and allow the Holy Spirit to examine for unbelief? Unbelief can cause you to be aloof from the living God. If you allow the Word of God to soak up all the unbelief and doubt, then you will know the truth and the truth will set you free.

Unbelief is as deadly as a poisonous snake. When it bites you, it makes you aloof toward the living God, and trusting to the god of this world—the devil. Who do you want defending you—the One who made you or that who was made by the One who made you?

A loving God has rest for an unfaithful bride, but because of unbelief, He cannot give out His rest to the bride. He keeps persuading mankind to give them rest. Some accept it unconditionally, while others put conditions on His love and fall into the web of unbelief. Like the Internet holds a multitude of Web sites, there are many web sites of unbelief.

One such Web site is that of other tongues. Some don't believe that other tongues are for today, but our Lord said that those who believe would speak with other tongues. Our Lord said this! This is not some doctrine made up by part of the Body of Christ, Our Lord Jesus said those who believe would speak with other tongues. If Jesus is the same yesterday, today, and forever more, then we have problems in the Body of Christ. Either Jesus is not the same forever, or He is the same forever. If He is the same forever, that means that what He spoke in the Bible is for us today. See this one subject has many of my brothers and sisters operating in unbelief or disobedience. Jesus gave the Body of Christ, His Church, a way to communicate with God the Father directly and over half the Body of Christ refuses to communicate this way because of unbelief. One verse says you are refreshed by speaking in tongues, yet another verse says you build up your most Holy faith by speaking in other tongues. Can you see how powerful this spirit of unbelief is? Can you see how it has choked the Body of Christ? Can you see the division this spirit has caused in the Body of Christ?

Unbelief can destroy a vision. Jesus gave His Church a weapon (The Holy Spirit) and only half of the Church realize the importance of this powerful weapon. Why is this so? The answer is that unbelief is among us. Open your spiritual eyes and see the trick of the devil. He wants unbelief in the Body of Christ—the Blood-purchased Church. A house divided cannot stand. That is the reason the Church is not as powerful today as it was in the days of Peter and Paul.

Which Web site of unbelief are you operating in? I will not make a list, as I do not want to miss your area of unbelief and therefore give you ground to excuse yourself. Take it seriously and ask the Holy Spirit to examine your heart. Is the Web site of unbelief such a great place to be? Remember this one very important thing: you are going against God when you operate in unbelief and doubt. Don't stay in the land of unbelief. God's land of milk and honey is waiting for you when you get into belief. Israel spent forty years in the desert on what could have been an eleven day journey because of unbelief. If you were born between 1946 and 1964 you belong to what has been called the baby boomers generation. You don't have forty years to stay in the desert of unbelief. Jesus could come back any day for His Church. He did not say that He would find unbelief when He returns, He said that He will find faith on the earth when He returns. Unbelief is a killer! The one who came to kill, steal, and destroy is the devil.

Chapter Six

The Sign of Holiness

The sign of holiness is not outward appearance. The sign of holiness is walking in faith in everything you do. Faith means obedience. Obedience means faithfulness in doing what the Word says. Do not spend your life wondering what God is going to do. If you can read, you should know what He is going to do. He is going to confirm the words of Matthew, Mark, Luke, and John. God is not going to write any new books of the Bible for you. You can have your own doctrine if you want to, but nothing but God's is successful. If you are not successful, do not blame God; there is nothing wrong with Him. Blame yourself. The Bible is never wrong. Jesus is never wrong. Check up on why you are not enjoying the blessings of God. God does not honor wondering. He honors faith. Nothing is too difficult or too hard for the Lord. Every bad thing that happens is the work of Hell, but the work of Hell has to bow to the authority of the name of Jesus.

A person involved with addictions, perversion, or compulsions will eventually lose his mind. He will lose all self-respect. If you give your life to the Lord Jesus Christ, keep your body full of the Holy Spirit, and praise the name of Jesus, your mind will never snap. Your body is the temple of the Holy Spirit. God wants you to have a sound mind, a mind full of peace, power, love and joy.

Do not allow yourself to be satisfied with anything except total victory. Read John 3:16–21, and see that holiness is the best way to victory in your life. Without it, you will never please God. With it, you will always please God. Mark, Matthew, Luke, and John all pointed us to the Person of holiness, the Lord Jesus Christ. It is sad that the world is without Jesus. Can you picture a son growing up without a father to guide and direct him? That is what we choose when we will not accept Jesus' holiness.

The very One who died so the world could lived is not wanted in about 3 billion homes on this planet. Many do not believe that holiness is profitable. I challenge you to check out what unholiness has brought to the table: cancer for one, aids for another, two of the worst diseases going in this world. Both arrived on the planet because of the residents desire to practice unholiness on earth. God is a holy God and desires for his people to be holy. God does not accept anything else.

The sign that lets you know that you are practicing holiness is obedience. Without it, you can not get very far in the Kingdom of God. Obedience to the Word of God is a must in order to achieve greatness in the Kingdom of God. Jesus said that greatness in the Kingdom of God is obtained by being a servant. Well if you are not obedient to the Word of God you can not be a servant. The two work hand-in-hand!

If you are not a servant, most likely the sign of holiness is not operating in your life. Holiness and obedience are twins; one cannot operate without the other. God the Father is just like any earthly father. If you are not obedient to your earthly father, he will not reward you. Likewise, if you are not obedient to your Heavenly Father He will not reward you. Without the spirit of obedience in your life, you cannot obtain holiness. The price that you must paid for holiness runs through the station of obedience.

The station of obedience can be a long station or a short station. You determine what the layout is going to be. If you determine that obedience is not something that you really want, then the station of obedience is going to be short. If you determine that obedience is something that you really want, then the station of obedience is going to be long, and the reward eternal.

I met a godly man who, after several years of being in the prison system, decided that the station of obedience and the reward was something that he was going to get. After many years in the system of Satan, he made an escape to the land of obedience, and has never looked back. His decision to be obedient rather than disobedient has caused him to soar above the land of disobedience. He now lands and takes off from the landing strip of obedience airport. He can now see the runway when he takes off and when he lands. Holiness has caught him, and will not let him go free. He now seeks holiness, after so many years of seeking unholiness. Jesus is his Lord and his Father is God. The Holy Spirit who directs him and guides him has replaced Satan. He no longer is guided by the angels of darkness, but by the angels of lightness. I want to express the fact that obedience is the key factor to holiness. Following in the steps of a Holy God is holiness. Doing as God says in His Word produced holiness. The choice is yours! What do you want in life? Holiness brings blessings, while unholiness brings curses.

God said that whosoever believes in His Son shall never perish, but have everlasting life. Not just life, but everlasting life. That means that the life will last forever. In the natural, life will not last forever and forever. Life will never cease to end if you believe in the Son of God. What a simple promise! But so many people have missed the boat and never believed in the Son of God. Why have they not believed in the Son of God? The answer is very simple: Deception of Satan.

The Word of God says he deceived the whole world. It is better to be obedient. God is looking for those who will be obedient to His Word and to His shepherds. Another key of holiness is peace. My son has really taken advantage of my wife and me, but God has given us his peace that allows us to continue to love him without wrath. God's love will give you peace.

What is holiness? The Vines says that holiness is pure from evil conduct and observant of God's will. God's will brings peace in your life know matter what the situation looks like. Although our son has caused us hurt we still love him as if nothing has happened. The peace of God continued to overtake us each and every day. Again I say, "My God is a faithful God." Holiness can be described as characteristically godliness. God is a God of peace and we are to act like Him. God did not worry when Samson fell, and He will not worry when we fall.

Peace is a sign of holiness. We practice what the Father is like, and God will reward us openly. Everyone will know that the hand of God is on your life when you operate in the peace of God. You can't help but to attract others when the peace of God is operating in your life. Jesus did not die on the cross for fear to control you; He died on the cross for peace to control you. Jesus says that the peace He gives, the world can not give or take away (John 14:27). That unspeakable peace is a sign of holiness. When you operate in the unspeakable peace of God; you operate in the blessings of God. If you are operating in the blessings of God then they will overtake you sooner or later.

Step up to the plate of life; don't let holiness to strike you out. You must get a hit off of holiness in order to continue in the anointing of God. Holiness is waiting for you to get a hit in life. We have discussed two elements of holiness. One is obedience and the other is peace? Without peace there is no obedience and without obedience there is no peace. Peace is a vital key to holiness, without peace you will never give what has been freely given to you.

The Lord enables you more and more to spend your lives in the interests of others, in order that He may so establish you in Christian character now, that you maybe vindicated from every charge that might possibly be brought against you at the Judgment seat of Christ. One day, all of us must stand before the Judgment seat of Christ. Everyone must play the game of life.

No one gets to go to the head of the class without first playing the game of life. Each of us must first play life's game. Each of us must first operate in the peace of God in order to obtain the prize of holiness. The prize of holiness awaits each person who can conquer it. Each person who operates in the wisdom of God will operate in the peace of God. Holiness is reflected in Christian character. If you obtain a life of holiness, every prize that accompanies holiness comes along.

Chapter Seven

Confirming to This World, or To Christ

In Romans 12:1–2, Paul the Apostle makes an appeal to brethren to not be conformed to this world. Today this appeal is still open to all Christians to not be conformed to this world. What are they conforming to? Christians are conforming to external, superficial customs. What customs of this world have you claimed as your own? Are you leaving work a few minutes early and using the excuse that everyone else does the same thing? Well, if you are a Christian, you are not everyone else. You belong to the Lord Jesus, and when you go to work you are working for the Lord Jesus. Your boss is only a stand in for your true Boss—the Lord Jesus Christ.

You may have never thought of it like that, but you are conforming to the world. This may seem minor to you, but one day you will have to give an account to your real Boss—the Lord Jesus Christ. An guess what He is going to say to you, concerning you leaving work a few minutes early because "everyone else does it"? He is going to say did you know that you worked for Me? If you answer No Sir, He will remind you that all things was made by Him for Him. Do you fit into that category? Let review what Paul said in Romans 12:1–2:

I appeal to you therefore, brethren, and beg of you in view of (all) the mercies of God, to make a decisive dedication of your bodies (presenting all your members and faculties) as a living sacrifice,holy (devoted, consecrated) and well pleasing to God, which is your reasonable (rational, intelligent) service and spiritual worship. Do not be conformed to this world (this age), (fashioned after and adapted to its external, superficial customs), but be transformed (changed) by the (entire) renewal of your mind (by its new ideals and its new attitude), so that you may prove (for yourselves) what is the good and acceptable and perfect will of God, even the thing which is good and acceptable and perfect (in His sight, for you).

Paul was appealing for us not to get caught up in a superficial world. I believe with all my heart that God knows mankind must be devoted to something in order to live. If we are devoted to the superficial things of this world, we miss out on the true riches of the Kingdom of Heaven. We cannot serve two masters. The Word of God says we will either love one and hate the other.

Stop and think for one second! Conforming to this world is the wrong way to go. This world is not on your side at all. Again, think about this world for a second. Christians and non-Christians alike are attacked in this world by the devil and his demons. There is no sickness in Heaven where God lives. There is sickness in Hell, whose primary occupant will be the devil when his lease is up. When man fell and the devil became the landlord of this world, he brought sickness with him as well as all of the devilish things that come with him. I beg of you like Paul do not be conformed to this world with its superficial customs? Believe, Believe, Believe, the Word of God!

Ever since we became members of our Church here in Sacramento, California, my wife and I have strived to renew our minds so that we can be devoted to God. Believe me, the benefits of the renewal of your mind are greater then the benefit of fashioning and adapting your self to the world's external, superficial customs. The choice is yours. If you choose to conform yourself to the world in reality you have chose death.

The prince of the air—the devil, runs this world. If you choose to transform your mind by its new ideals and its new attitude you have chose life. God is life! One Scripture says For in Him we live and move and have our being (Acts 17:28). The reality of life is that without Christ Jesus, you are nothing and can do not one thing, but in Christ Jesus you are somebody and can do all things. The battlefield is your mind. This world is after you all the time.

My main concern is to please God. How do I please God? The only way that I know is by being obedient. That is what Jesus did when He walked the earth. He was obedient! How do I learn obedience? This is an easy question to answer. The Word of God!

I have forgiven my son. Do you want to know how I knew that I had forgiven him? Well one day he came to my work unexpected. I was looking at him face to face, and even those he still didn't seem to be truly sorry about what had taken place, I wasn't angry. My job is to forgive.

Jesus said in the Word of God that if we do not forgive others, our Father in Heaven cannot forgive us. This world does not forgive others. It may say it does, but it doesn't. God's forgiveness is also forget. We are to forgive and forget. I do not mean that you forget that the incident took place, but when you see the person, you do not hold the person's offense against them.

That's why your mind needs to be renewed by the Word of God. If you don't forgive; the Father can't forgive you. If God can't forgive you, then you have open all the doors for the devil and his demons to attack you. You have tied God's protective hands! Is it really worth the trouble to stay mad at someone? Romans 12:1–2 are very important verses! Study them, and get them into your spirit.

Even though my wife and I had great trouble with the Credit Bureau, my son's actions did not give me the right to operate in unforgiveness. God forgave us when we were still sinners! If the Creator of the universe can offer forgiveness and let His Son die for us, then who are we to say that we cannot forgive one another? Do not be conformed to this world. We do not have the right to refuse to forgive anyone for their hurtful actions toward us. Believe the Word of God today. If you have been in the habit of not believing the Word of God, I want to urge you to change your attitude to one of belief today. Believe, Believe, Believe, and you shall receive. If you are a Christian, it is your reasonable service to transform your mind. If you are not a Christian I beg you to please allow Jesus to become the Lord and Savior of your life. Romans 10:9 says, Because if you acknowledge and confess with your lips that Jesus is Lord and in your heart believe (adhere to, trust in, and rely on the truth) that God raised Him from the dead, you will be saved.

Pray the above confess over your life and over the lives of all your loves ones. Up until the point of salvation, you were one of the living dead. Your spirit was dead, Through salvation, you have moved into eternal life. What does this world have to offer you? It offers murder, stealing, adultery, lying, cheating, fornication, jealousy, and covetousness. All of these proceed from the mouth of the devil. Not one of the categories can be labeled as from God. Every person can claim at least one of these as his own. If you are operating in any of these areas, you have just got a taste of what it means to be conformed to this world. It is easy to be a citizen of this world rather than a citizen of the Kingdom of Heaven.

Back to my son—my wife forgave him as well. Since we are one, then God forgives us both. Think about this husband and wife: God sees you as one. If one forgives and the other one does not, you are in danger of blocking forgiveness from God. A husband and a wife must be on one accord to experience the fullness of God in their marriage, family, and in all that they do. Everything that you do must be good, acceptable, and mature in the sight of God for you. This is word that need to be repeated over and over. Everything that you do must be good, acceptable, and mature in the sight of God. Do not be foolish! Whatever a man sows, that he will reap. The Bible is given to us for reproof and for instruction. If you want to know the good, acceptable, and mature will of God it is written for you.

Some people think if they do not know what God expects of them, they are not accountable, but God does not operate like that. Since He gave His only begotten Son and His Word. We are accountable! That is the main reason the devil and his demons fight so hard to keep us in darkness. You are accountable! Your accountability started the day you were born. Even if you've never opened a Bible, you are still accountable. That is the reason why it doesn't pay to ignore what the Word of God says and what Jesus' blood accomplished.

Each person will be judged! God can judge each person, because each is accountable to find out what the Word says about the good, acceptable, and mature will of God. This book is written to each person on earth. It is not just for Christians! Regardless of their choices or religion, each person is accountable to stand before God, to be judged on that great day to see if they proved in their life the good, acceptable, and perfect Will of God for them. The Creator of the universe will call you before Him to see how you have lived out your life. It is important that you do not conform to this world. This world does not have your future in mind. That plan can come only from the one who made you.

The devil doesn't know what it is that God has planned for us, though he does know that there is a plan for us, because before his fall, he was in heaven and knows the heart of God toward his people. Satan, too, had been created with a purpose, a God-given life plan, which he chose to reject.

Since the devil knows from experience that there is a plan for your life, he does all that he can to cause you to get off the road of life, and into the ditch of life. I want to bring to light the slow, but careful plan the devil has for your life. He is a master of distractions! Every distraction that he can place in front of you takes you further and further into the ditch of life. So when the day of accountability comes, you will be in trouble, because you never got back on the road of life. You drove all the way in the ditch, never knowing you could at anytime gotten back on the road. The devil deserves an Oscar for his star performance for keeping people off the road of life.

In God there is a good, acceptable, and perfect will for each of us. Our job is to find it. The devil's job is to distract us from pursuing it. Who is going to win?

Many people have come through the road of life and have not found God's will for their life. Those who have found His will have been successful in life. I am not judging success like you'd think. Some of these people were wealthy and some were poor. What they had in common was that when they stood before the Lord, the will of God for their lives lined up with the road of life they were on. They were identical, nothing missing, nothing broken. The will for their lives was what the Father chose for them. I am closing this chapter with these statements: You cannot afford not to be transformed by the renewing of your mind with the Word of God. You cannot afford not to search out the will of God, for your life. You must not be conformed to this world!

Chapter Eight

Believe What You Are

In order to have what you want, you must believe what you are. You must be believe that you are a child of God in Christ. Most Christians do not know who they are. Being a child of Christ is a special benefit that belongs to you. You are a somebody—not just a sinner saved by grace. In Christ, there is divine favor. Favor that overtakes you were every you go. Favor that opens doors for you. Favor that makes your job application stand out among others. Favor that tells your boss that you deserve a raise. Favor that determines that when a new position comes up, you are considered before anyone else. Favor that goes from you to your children in everything that they do. Divine favor goes before you to prepare the way! You are in Christ. In Christ, there are benefits that set you apart from the world. You are in the world, but you are not part of the world. You must believe that you are in Christ. Satan's job is to make you believe that you are not in Christ. Many Christians don't know who they are. You have been removed from one Kingdom and placed into another Kingdom.

I recall telling a senior citizen once that we were removed from the kingdom of the devil and placed in the Kingdom of God. This gentlemen said that the devil does not have a kingdom. Many people believe that statement, though God says that the devil has a kingdom.

Being strengthened with all power according to his glorious might so that you may have great endurance and patience, and joyfully giving thanks to the Father, who has qualified you to share in the inheritance of the saints in the kingdom of light. For he has rescued us from the dominion of darkness and brought us into the kingdom of the Son he loves, in whom we have redemption the forgiveness of sins (Col. 1:11-14).

This senior citizen friend of mine loved God, but he had never read in the Bible that the devil has a Kingdom. What a shame!

This gentleman could have helped many people if he had known the truth concerning the kingdom of the devil. I say that because millions of people are in the kingdom of the devil right now. Sadly, they do not know they are in the kingdom of the devil. Which kingdom do you belong to? You may say that you belong to the Kingdom of Light, but do you believe what you are?

God says you are a new creation in Christ, in Christ you have everything you need for life and you are His witness and His workmanship. If you are a new creation; then you do not have a past. How can a new creation that was just made have a past? Stop beating yourself up! If God says you are a new creation, believe Him. You do not have to live in the shame of your past, you have the right to a bright future.

Stop! Stop! Stop! If you are a believer you do not have to be condemned for your past. Believe what you are. A child of God; a new creation, made in the image of the Father and a joint heir with Jesus Christ. You are not just Gwen, Larry, Martha, or George; you are a child of the Most High God. This is awesome the Most High God is your Father! The one who made the universe has chosen you to be His child. What an honor to be chosen by the Most High God! That is why the devil wants to keep you from knowing who you are in Christ. A person who finds out who they are in Christ is dangerous to the Kingdom of the devil. When you believe what you are; you can receive what you are.

Believing and receiving go hand in hand in the process of knowing what you are in Christ Jesus. You will never advance in the things of God without first believing and then receiving. You have been selected before the foundation of the world to be what you are: A child of God in Christ Jesus! There is no other title fitting. Child of the Most High God.

Satan is doing all he can to keep believers from knowing what they are in Christ Jesus. We are nothing without Christ, but everything in Christ. We can do all things in Christ Jesus. See the importance of knowing what you are in Christ? Without knowing who you are you go the down the wrong path of life and never fulfill God's plan for your life.

"For I know the plans I have for you," declares the lord, "plans to prosper you and not to harm you, plans to give you hope and a future. Then you will call upon me and come and pray to me, and I will listen to you" (Jer.29:11, 12).

The one who is happy about you never fulfilling the plan for your life is the devil, because he did not have to put up much of a fight to keep you off your designed path that God plan for you. Through your spiritual laziness you never persuaded God to find out what plan He designed for you. Stop! Let me tell you how you can get His plan for your life. Are you ready? Pray and fast; getting away from everyone and spend time alone with God. You will not only find out who you are in Christ, but what plan God has designed for your life.

Being alone with God, praying and fasting will get you your answers. I took that time away and found out that I was to write books. You are reading the first of those books, and are experiencing a part in the plan God mapped out for my life. I went some twenty-six years after High School graduation before finding out that I was a writer. I never saw myself as a writer; but God saw me as a writer. I never saw myself as a minister; but God saw me as a minister. It is up to me to believe and receive what God says I am.

You can't hear the voice of God in front of the TV. God speaks to your spirit, so your spirit must be in tune with His Spirit to know what you are in Christ Jesus. The old James Lincoln did not know he was a writer, but the new creation does. The old James did not have a future, but the new James does. The old James had a past that could haunt him, but the new James is free.

If we don't believe what God says, then we judge God a liar—God is not a man that He lies or the Son of man that He repents. I am a new creation and old things have passed away. Believe, Believe, Believe, what and who you are in Christ Jesus and all of the Kingdom of Heaven will belong to you. If you have not made Jesus your Lord, you must confess with your mouth that Jesus is Lord and believe in your heart that God raised Jesus from the dead and you will be saved. After you ask Jesus into your heart, you must be obedient to the Word of God.

In the course of time Cain brought some of the fruits of the soil as an offering to the LORD.

But Abel brought fat portions from some of the firstborn of his flock. The LORD looked with favor on Abel and his offering, but on Cain and his offering he did not look with favor. So Cain was very angry, and his face was downcast.

Then the LORD said to Cain, "Why are you angry? Why is your face downcast? If you do what is right, will you not be accepted? But if you do not do what is right, sin is crouching at your door; it desires to have you, but you must master it" (Gen. 4:3-7).

Obedience is what made Abel's offering more acceptable to God than Cain's. Abel was obedient to what he was told! We must be obedient to the Word of God if we are to walk in the things of God and receive the things in Christ. If you believe; you will be obedient and if you are obedient you will believe. Obedience will cause you to believe what you are in Christ Jesus.

The author of the Bible is God Himself. The Holy Spirit of God uses men, but the author is God Himself. I am one of those people who believes the Word of God—if God says it, then it is so. If you choose not to believe what

God says about you then you are in unbelief. The Word of God is very important and must be studied.

Strong's defines the word receive as to take into one's possession. If you don't believe what you are in Christ Jesus; you can't take into your possession what you are in Christ Jesus. The battle is half over, because all the devil has to do now is delay you from having what rightfully belongs to you.

The devil does not really have to defeat you; all he got to do is delay you from possessing what is rightfully yours in the first place. Until you claim a gift it is not yours! Wake up, Body of Christ! We are at war and have been for over 2000 years.

The devil's plan is delay, delay, and delay. Get this: he is a defeated foe. If he is a defeated foe and he is; why is he keeping so many brothers and sisters rightfully goods from them? The answer is delays. A weapon of the devil; used against The Body of Christ.

The Body of Christ does not overall believe what we are in Christ Jesus. We are powerless though Christ Jesus gave all power to us. So what is the deal? Christ Jesus gave all power to us and we act like we are defenseless babes. We are not believing and receiving what and who we are in Christ Jesus. Again, the word receive means to take into one's possession. If you don't believe in it, you can't take hold of it.

It is that simple! A fallen angel is calling the shots against people who are made in the image of the Almighty God. Many are living as if Jesus is never going to return. Many are taken God's mercy for granted. Many believers are living with the chickens; when they should be living with the eagles. Many believers deny themselves the power of God. Many are playing church instead of being the Church. The word Church means the called-out ones. Wake up Body of Christ you were called out! Called out of darkness.

Each person who is born on this earth arrives in the Kingdom of darkness. Our first parents (Adam and Eve) sinned against God. At that point, they received a sinful nature and that nature as been passed down from generation to generation ever since that awful day. Before they sinned, our first parents had a godly nature. In order to get a godly nature; everyone must be born again. God is a just God; a loving God. He made a way for us to get rid of that sinful nature: Through the blood of His Son, Christ Jesus. We have everything we need for life in Christ Jesus.

Jesus made everything for Himself. If we abide in Him and He abides in us, then everything we need for life will be given to us in Christ Jesus. We live and move and have our being in Christ Jesus. If I have everything I need for life in Christ Jesus; but do not believe it or lay hold of it, then I am still powerless. I can't take possession of the things I need for life if I don't believe. My purpose for this book is to encourage each person to study the Bible like they have never studied any other book before.

In the 66 Chapters of the Bible lays all you need for life. God wrote a plan that if followed with obedience you would reach the top of the mountain of God with everything you need in life provided for you free of charge. Everything you need is stored in the Book of Instruction.

You can't find another book with the instructions obtained in the Bible. The Most High God wrote the book! Since the Most High God wrote the book and the Body of Christ are children of the Most High God don't you think we should take possession of the Word and rewards it as to offer. Everything I need in life and everything you need in life is within the covers of the most talked about book in the world. Revelation knowledge of how to live your life is in the Word of God. Who and what you are; is spelled out so plain for you. In Christ is freedom that most of the world will never know.

I encourage you to spend at least 15 minutes a day reading the Bible. You will be amazed at your growth in the Word. If you profess to be a Christian, yet find full satisfaction in worldly pleasures and pursuits, your profession is faulty. Too many people make the mistake of measuring the certainty of their salvation by their feelings instead of the facts of God's Word. In Jesus Christ you have a New Life. You must know your position! Another way of putting it—believe what you are! We are His witness and His workmanship. He is working in us to produce the fruit of the Spirit in our lives. For one purpose—to be a witness for Him.

If we yield to the Holy Spirit; we can produce fruit in our lives, but only when we yield to the Holy Spirit. The Holy Spirit will make alive what we are in Christ Jesus once we have yielded ourselves to Him. It is Jesus working in us, not we in ourselves that make us witnesses for Him, equipped to take the gospel unto the entire world.

Examine yourself! Where are you in your relationship with the Lord? Are you in position? Or are you out of position? If you are in position—stay. If you are out of position—get back where you belong. Examine yourself and see if any unbelief is trapped in your heart. This chapter has been the most fun chapter for me to write. If you get in position and believe what you are in Christ and receive what you are in Christ, you get to the top. I will see you at the top.

Chapter Nine

True Repentance

The conversion of Saul in Acts 9:1–20 can be labeled as true repentance. Saul, who had murdered Christians and was on a journey to murder more, was stopped in his tracks after an encounter with the risen Lord. Saul went from being Saul, enemy of the Lord to being Paul, apostle of the Lord. He truly changed his ways, thoughts, and patterns of life.

Repentance is going from one direction and to another. In Acts 9:1–20, you see that he did not keep the same friends. In order for true repentance to come about in your life you must change your friends. If your friends have been saved and redeemed as well, that is fine, but if they have not, let them alone. That old stuff does not belong to you anyway, because you have a future in Christ. Also in Acts 9:1–20, Saul fell to the ground and heard a voice. He did not try to stay up and hear the voice of the Lord.

Saul also asked, "what do you want me to do?" Most people try to stay in control, instead of letting God have control of their lives. They do not even try to hear what the voice of the Lord is saying to them. At the present time my only daughter falls into that category. She will not want to stay there, but because of spiritual laziness she does not hear the voice of the Lord.

Saul falling to the ground was symbolic of yielding to the Lord. Once Saul yielded to the Lord, he was able to hear the voice of the Lord. Saul was not saved at the time the Lord spoke to him. In fact, Saul can be labeled as a religious person. He knew a lot about God, but he did not know God. I can estimate that over half the Body of Christ can be labeled like Saul. Knowing about someone, and knowing them are not the same. Knowing some means you know their heart, what they like, what they do not like and they know you the same way. If you are not spending time with God personally then He is not spending time with you personally.

When you spend time with someone, you get to know him or her on a personal basis. You begin to know everything about them. God is no different. He is our Father and we must know Him as our Father. Saul was a man well-educated in religion. In fact, Saul studied under the most popular teachers of his time. He was not only educated, but very devoted to Israel's religion. Still, he was off track to say the least; killing and hunting Christians because he thought they where wrong for believing in Jesus or His ways.

Christianity was not called Christianity then; the disciples of Jesus were radically different than the rest of their society. They were "in the way." What a special name, because Jesus is the way to everything in life.

If you don't think there is a God, just look at Saul's life. He was on his way to jail disciples, and God jailed him for the Kingdom of God. Saul, who became Paul after his true repentance was nothing like Saul. He truly changed his ways, thoughts, and patterns of life. Paul died defending the same thing that he killed others for: The way!

Now as he traveled on, he came near to Damascus, and suddenly a light from Heaven flashed around him. And he fell to the ground. Then he heard a voice saying to him, "Saul, Saul, why are you persecuting (harassing, troubling, and molesting) Me?" And Saul said, "Who are You, Lord?" And He said, "I am Jesus, Whom you are persecuting" (Acts 9:3–5).

Paul had heard of Jesus, but never knew Jesus as the Son of God. What caused Saul to change his mind about Jesus? Saul did not change his mind. Jesus changed Saul's mind. Lets look at another Scripture. Acts 9:20: And immediately in the synagogues he proclaimed Jesus, saying, "He is the Son of God." Paul had true repentance, not half, but a whole change of lifestyle.

Can you imagine what the disciples thought about Saul? He was on a mission to kill them one minute, and then he wanted to love them. The Lord used Paul to write most of the New Testament. He was so yielded to the Holy Spirit that Paul overcame all the mistrust people had in him, and became one of the greatest disciples of the Lord that every lived. Paul never looked back at his past, expecting to be able to fix it. He realized that after that day on the road to Damascus, his past belonged to Jesus. Many of us in the Body of Christ need to have an Damascus experience. Paul never let Saul come to life again. He always remembered that it was not him, but Jesus living in him that did the work. Too many of us do not remember that Jesus lives in us. If you have the true repentance experience you will remember that Jesus lived in you and that you have been bought with the wonderful blood of Jesus. He paid a price just to get you back in relationship with the Father. The only thing that you can do to repay is to allow true repentance to have free course in your life.

We have been covering a lot about true repentance, but what is true repentance? Jesus said, if you love me you will follow my word. The word of Jesus is in the Bible. If you do not read the Bible you won't know the Word of the Lord. So you will be doing things that are not acceptable to the Lord or that fall in line with true repentance.

Again my daughter comes to mind; she accompanies us to church each Sunday, but I have yet to see her reading her Bible or spending time with God. Is this a sign of true repentance? The answer is no! Like so many young adults, she seems to think there is time to serve the Lord, but right now the world is calling. Young people, please do not fall for the lies of the devil. Remember, true repentance is changing from one way and going another way. Not much in the life of my daughter has changed at this point—she didn't read the Word or spend time with God before she made the confession to the Lord, nor does she at this point? Is there a true heart-repentance going on here? She is just like a lot of us, we have made a verbal confession like the Word says, but have not made a heart-confession like the Word says. We have only half way converted to Christ. Half of a conversion is not enough to keep you from being run over by the devil and demons. You need all of Christ to stay untouched by the evil one.

Jesus prayed that the evil one would not touch us. How many of you, brothers and sisters in Christ, know that Jesus prayed for you? You might say, I know Jesus is praying for me. That is true, but how many of you know that Jesus prayed for you when He was on earth? Read John 17, and you will find that Jesus prayed for all believers: those around back then and all those who would hear there words and become believers—you and me.

When you are born-again you change from one direction to another. We strive (or should) for true repentance—not fornicating again. True repentance—not stealing again. True repentance—not taking the shopping cart from the grocery store. True repentance—not taking pens from work.

True repentance does not commit adultery. True repentance does not bear false witness against its neighbor. True repentance does not gossip. True repentance does not cut people off driving. True repentance does not think of itself more highly then it does others. True repentance devotes time and energy to knowing the Lord choosing to associate with other believers rather than be unduly influenced by the world's values.

True repentance seeks reconciliation and healing in the family rather than divorce. True repentance accepts and supports those God has set in authority in the church. True repentance will refuse to enter legal action against a fellow believer. True repentance accepts any loss in order to secure or maintain right relationships in the family or the church and commits them to God for His restoration and reparation. True repentance relies totally on God for spiritual wisdom, rejecting the wisdom of the world. True repentance acknowledged our adoption as a child of God, calling Him "Father."

True repentance believes steadfastly that God will fulfill everything He has promised in His Word. True repentance can be summarized in three words: love, obedience, and unity. By living godly lives, we learn to see things as God does, and adopt His Word as our only standard. Adopting His Word as our only standard is true repentance in a nutshell. We prove our repentance by adopting His Word as our only standard. We do not have any other standard before us.

Obeying Jesus is the primary evidence that we love Him and are His disciples. Our decision to obey is the key to understanding the spiritual reality of the Scriptures, and frees the Holy Spirit to teach us. The Holy Spirit is our Teacher, Helper, Advocate, and Guide. He is our source of true spiritual understanding. He lifts up Jesus and builds up believers, enabling them to live the Christian life.

The glory of God is revealed to those who believe. To see the glory of God you must Believe, Believe, Believe. Why would God show you His glory if you do not believe? Recognize that the Kingdom of God requires your highest commitment. Understand that the Kingdom is worth more than any other pursuit. Be ready to forsake any personal goal that hinders your entering into it. Recognize that Kingdom people are childlike (not childish) in their faith and trust. Pursue child likeness in all your interpersonal dealings. True repentance—will suspect things that are popular or favored by the world-minded majority. Be warned that what you practice demonstrates our relationship with Jesus. Remember that popularity and human approval do not necessarily indicate God's approval of a situation. Understand that God's Kingdom authority and the world's systems of authority are often opposites. Put your treasures where you want your life to be. True repentance will keep you in line with the will of God for your life. True Repentance will not leave a hidden place in your heart untouched. True repentance will coverall the bases and make a home run for Jesus in your life.

Chapter Ten

Believe God's Prophets

Believe God's Prophets and you shall prosper. This is a promise from God Himself. Many people do not believe in and trust the pastor whose authority they are under. If the pastor you are under in your local church is an anointed man of God, then you have the promise of God for prosperity.

The Word is specific in this area. Second Chronicles 20: 20b, says Believe in the Lord your God and you shall be established; believe His prophets and you shall prosper.

The man of God may tell you to do something that does not seem right to the natural mind, but if it is not sin, your job is to do what he says. Our Man of God said to jump up and down. Well to the natural mind that did not seem right. In 2 Chronicles 20, the prophet of God told the army of Israel to sing and praise God going into battle.

For the natural mind that might not seem correct: In battle you fight, you don't usually go around singing and praising. However, the blessing that accompanied the people that believed the prophet of God was healing in their bodies. God does not tell you something that you can't do or that you will not receive a blessing from doing. He is always looking out for His children. Always trying to get a blessing into your hands. Think about that for a minute—you are in church and your pastor tells everyone to start jumping. That's not something that happens in a church. But remember, God, who made a wall fall down because some people walked around it seven times when they were told to can do all things and will do all things.

His prophets are His tools! The tools that God used can be small, big, white, brown, black, yellow, a man or a woman. They can be an educated tool or an uneducated tool. God just needs a willing vessel to get the job done. A willing vessel is also an obedient vessel. I have heard of a woman who believed what her pastor said, and began to share it with her employer. This woman was the housemaid of a wealthy woman. One day, this wealthy woman got convicted by God to do something for her housemaid and brought her a home costing 1 million dollars. This housemaid prospered behind her sharing what the man of God was teaching at her church. Can you see someone buying you a house that cost 1 million dollars and giving it to you?

When you believe God's prophets and let others know that you do you don't know what that will do to others. The conviction of God can come all over that person and caused them to bless you like you never imagine. You will always prosper if you believe God's prophets. Why can I say that? Because of God. Believe God's prophets and you shall prosper.

There are other stories in the Body of Christ of men and women prospering because they believed the prophet of God. A famous preacher of today saw a woman teaching about the Holy Spirit, and because of her, found the Holy Spirit for himself. He did not prosper financially, but the prospered spiritually. Today he is being used around the world; the Lord working with him to set the captive free. The choice this man made in Pittsburgh was the wisest choice he could have ever made. Many lives have been touched because he heard the prophet teaching about the Holy Spirit.

Another famous man of God heard about healing and took healing to the nation. Many people that would have died are alive because of him.

God's Prophets are not just for you, but for all those you come into contact with. When you go to church don't listen to the message just for you; listen to the message for others. Listen to the man of God with a heart to become a doer of the Word, and not a hearer only.

Who is God's Prophet? A man or woman full of The Holy Spirit and faith. To hear from God you must be full of the Holy Spirit of God. The Word says God is a Spirit, and He speaks to us by our spirit. As well, you must have faith. God says to please Him, you must have faith. In fact, the Bible tells us that it is impossible to please God without faith.

Being full of the Holy Spirit will drive out everything that is not of God from within you. A person full of the Holy Spirit will spend time with God and develop a relationship with Him. You also should be full of the Holy Spirit so you can hear the Spirit of God when He speaks through his prophets. If you are not in tune with the Holy Spirit, you may miss something that God wants you to hear or have.

Believing God's Prophets can save your love ones. You must receive what the man of God is saying. If the man of God is speaking a blessing over your love ones and they are not present in the audience, you can receive it for them. It may be for salvation, healing, or other kinds of blessings. Believe the prophet, and receive and share a blessing with your love ones.

Not everything that God does is just for you. In the Kingdom of God, blessings abound to all people. Recently, the Man of God who directs our House told us that God wanted to proclaim a fast —he called it Thirty-One Days of Glory.

If you do not hook up with what the Man of God has spoken, you could cause yourself to miss out on the blessings that will come in response to your obedience in believing God's Prophet. Our pastor wasn't speaking nonsense; God told him to declare a church-wide fast for the month of July. The assignment from God was an anointing to fast. God does not give you an assignment without equipping you to complete it.

Those who have said that they can't fast in reality don't want to fast. There was a certain king who believed the prophet Daniel (Dan.5). This king was not born again, but because he believed God's Prophet; God caused him to prosper. At first he did not have a personal relationship with God. God caused prosperity to fall upon this king because he believed Daniel. If you do not have a real man of God in your town, find one and attend his church. I mean a man who is full of faith and the Holy Spirit. He can't be half-and-half like the cream you put into coffee. He must be the real thing. A real man of God will cause you to grow in every area of your life. He will challenge you to live a holy life. If you have to travel 400 miles one way, do it. In the long run eternity is at stake. The price is too high to worry about driving 400 miles one way to church. Growth will overtake you! Because of your faithfulness; God is obligated to bless you in every area of your life.

Our church is in Sacramento, California and we have people who drive each and every Wednesday and Sunday from the Bay Area to church. They are blessed, and also are a blessing to others in the local Body of Christ here. The main reason that they make that drive each Wednesday and Sunday is that they believe God's prophet. A true sign of the validity of God's prophet is that you are growing in your personal relationship with God and in your personal life. If either of these are not happening, it might be a sign that either you are not really listening, or that the man is not a true prophet of God.

If you know the story of Peter, you will remember that Jesus told Peter, to feed his sheep. When you are fed, you grow. If you are not growing, examine were you have put down stakes. I do not mean to be critical of my brothers or sisters in the Body of Christ, but each of us should be growing in our relationship with the Lord. If you have not grown then you need to talk to the spiritual doctor, Jesus to find out what is affecting your spiritual growth. It just could be that you do not believe God's prophets. If the stakes you have laid down are across the pulpit of any of God's prophets, then you have a choice to go back and remove them.

You might say, "I haven't laid stakes down concerning my man of God, I just don't believe what he is saying came from God." If there is any fruit coming from the man of God's life, then you should know that he is God's prophet.

God told Moses to lead His people out of Egypt. When the Egyptians did not believe Moses, they were destroyed. God will not destroy you— but being distrustful of the man of God may cause doors around you to be closed to you. Goodness will come to you and you will not be able to see it. Favor will chase you down and you will not be able to know that it is looking you in the face. Why? Because when you do not believe God's prophets you take yourself out of the know.

The problem that is out of control in the Body of Christ today is a lack of belief, or trust in the man of God. Saints, our job is not to tell the man of God what to do. If you think that they are not hearing from God, then your job is to pray for them. When you don't do that you are posing as judge.

Therefore, you have no excuse or defense or justification, O man, whoever you are who judges and condemns another. For in posing as judge and passing sentence on another, you condemn yourself, because you who judge are habitually practicing the very same things (that you censure and denounce) (Rom. 2:1)

God is telling you do not judge and condemn another. Do not confuse misunderstanding and disbelief, they are different things. If you don't understand the prophet of God, go pray and ask God to reveal unto you what the man of God said. Do not just throw it aside and not believe what the man of God said. You can get yourself out of position operating in disbelief!

If the prophet of God tells you to run, get up and run. Do not just sit there letting the spirit of pride have its way in your life. You might not understand why he is telling you to run, but God knows, and He requires your obedience. At our church, we had a man of God who was visiting and he told a whole row of people to get up and run. The power of God hit each one and whatever they were believing God for, they got it, because of their obedience. That sounds silly to the natural mind—to run in church. Remember that God's ways are higher then our ways and His thoughts are higher then our thoughts.

Always operate in the spirit of belief! You will find blessings overtake you when you operate in the spirit of belief. The Prophet of God might not know why he is telling you to run, but he knows that at the end God has a reward waiting for you, if you will Believe, Believe, Believe.

Let every person be loyally subject to the governing (civil) authorities. For there is no authority except from God (by His permission, His sanction), and those that exist do so by God's appointment. Render to all men their dues.

(Pay) taxes to whom taxes are due, revenue to whom revenue is due, respect to whom respect is due, and honor to whom honor is due (Rom 13:5-7).

We can honor our man of God by paying for their support and believing what they preach. God tells us to give honor to whom honor is due. I can't think of another person to whom honor is due more than God's prophets. You honor them by believing and acting on the Word of God they deliver to you each time the doors of the church are open.

In the Body of Christ, the Pastor or Shepherd of the Church is the governing authority. We are to be loyal to the Pastor. Do not curse the man of God, just pray and ask God to reveal to you if you have missed the word, or ask the prophet of God if they have missed it.

I know I have been saying man, but it can be a woman also. In the book of Acts it talks about Philip's daughters who were prophetess. Why was the five-fold ministry gifts given by Jesus? The reason was to equip the saints. You can't be equipped if you do not believe what your instructor is telling you.

In a way, the prophet of God is an instructor telling you what the Lord Jesus wants you to learn so that you can be equipped to fight the devil and his demons, and be victorious in life. So the amount of victory that you experience in life is directly tied to how much you believe God's prophets. God tells us not to be just a hearer of the Word, but a doer of the Word. You can't say you are a doer of the Word if you do not believe the prophet of God. You shoot yourself in one foot and break the other foot. You are not operating in faith, because you do not believe God's prophet.

Satan comes quicker then you can say "shout" to steal the Word sown in your heart. If you do not believe the prophet then the Word you hear falls on hard and immovable ground. It does you no good. You just heard and did not take any action to apply it to your life. Why? Because you did not believe God's prophet. Yes, there are people who are not true prophets of God. You will know the true prophet; he or she is the one with all the fruit following them around. Not people following, but fruit following!

Their lifestyle is an example of Jesus. They talk like God and move like God. They are men or women who are blessed coming in, and blessed going out. They truly talk the talk, and walk the walk. When you are in their presence, you feel the presence of God.

God is producing men and women who will not compromise His Word in these last days. They are men or women whose lives are holy and blameless. They are men or women who are seeking God's heart with all their spirit, soul, mind, and thoughts.

True prophets of God do not boast of themselves, but their gifts bring them before great men. God's anointing is on their lives for greatness. All they touch with their hands brings glory to God. Do you know someone like this? If you are in their church great, if you are not, then find a true prophet of God, so the blessings of God can get to you more quickly.

I am not saying that God must use a prophet, but I am saying that some things that we want from God must come through the prophet of God hands. The anointing of God upon that prophet can work god's will in your life.

Chapter Eleven

The Dramatic Protection of the Lord

The Lord is our shield in times of trouble. You have all probably heard of the story of Shadrack, Meshach, and AbedNego, who were placed in the fiery furnace because of their faith in the Almighty God. The Scripture in Daniel describes the dramatic protection of the Lord like no other.

"Look," he answered, "I see four men loose, walking in the midst of the fire; and they are not hurt, and form of the fourth is like the Son of God" (Dan. 3:25).

Shadrack, Meshach, and AbedNego would not bow down to the enemy at all, and because of their courage, God came through in a dramatic way for them. Image how King Nebuchadnezzar felt when he saw four men instead of three men walking in the furnace! The faith that these men exhibited in the face of death is amazing. If each Christian would exhibit the same courage as these men, our world today would be completely saved. Because of their faith in God, the King ordered all the people to worship the God of Shadrack, Meshach, and AbedNego. The King also recognized that Shadrack, Meshach, and AbedNego trusted in God with all of their heart. This kind of trust will cause the devil to surrender all his captives immediately.

King Nebuchadnezzar called Shadrack, Meshach, and AbedNego servants of the Most High God. What the King was saying is that there is no other god but the Most High God who can deliver us from the power of fire. This same deliverance is available today because Jesus is the same yesterday, today, and forever more. God never changes!

If this protection is available today; why are we not hearing about Christians being delivered like Shadrack, Meshach, and AbedNego were? If this dramatic protection of the Lord is still available; how do Christians each and every day back down from the devil and his demons? The fiery furnace incident is just a taste of the protection God provides for His people.

One reason that we do not hear about incidents like the fiery furnace is that Christians over look the everyday protection of God and take it for granted. You may not be thrown into a furnace, but in this world you face situations of death each day.

My wife was driving on the freeway at 65 miles per hour; when her front tire went flat; God allowed her to get off the freeway onto the ramp without an incident or the car going out of control. She was not placed in a furnace, but her life was in danger; without the dramatic protection of the Lord it is possible that she would not be here today or seriously injured.

I was driving home from church, when a young girl suddenly appeared in front of my van; I did not have time to stop, but she was placed by on the sidewalk without being hurt at all. This was the dramatic protection of the Lord on the behalf of my family, that young girl, and myself. The Most High God never takes a break; He said that He will never leave you or forsake you! Jesus is on guard twenty-four seven. He is always watching out for His people.

Shadrach, Meshach and AbedNego were protected by God because they trusted in Him. They were not afraid to tell the King that they would not worship his god and that they would not stop praising their God. We must not be ashamed of the gospel of Jesus Christ, for it is the power to salvation. If you become bold like the three Hebrew men and trust in Him, there is no demon in Hell that can stop the power of God on your behalf.

Being placed into a furnace that is seven times more heated than it is usually is no joke. King Nebuchadnezzar was going to make sure that the three Hebrews were dead. Shadrach, Meshach, and AbedNego were on display; they had no time for weakness. They put it all on the line, trusting that their God would not only protect them, but deliver them. They were not a bunch of nutty fruit bars. They were real men! Real men not only love God, but they trust God with all their heart, mind, and soul.

The dramatic protection of the Lord is waiting for every born again believer to claim it. The Lord Jesus Christ punched your ticket at Calvary. All you've got to do now is get on the Train of Trust. A ride on The Train of Trust is not expensive, but is a one-way fare. There are no round trip tickets, because all the trains point directly to Jesus.

Jesus is our dramatic protection! All we need is in Him. I can think of many times when Jesus protected me while I was in the world rather than loving Him. In one instance, I was stationed at Scott Air Force Base, Illinois. I was driving on the freeway between East Saint Louis, Illinois and Belleville, Illinois.

I started to fall asleep and when I woke up I was in a ditch. Two young men were trying to get me to take my feet of the gas pedal. They told me that I had started off in in the far left lane of the six lane freeway, and started to come over one lane at a time. They told me that not one car had to stop to avoid hitting me, and that I finally reached the ditch.

They'd turned their vehicle around and came back to check on me. I was not saved at the time, but the dramatic protection of the Lord was focused on me. If I had died that night, I would not have fulfilled God's plan for my life. What myself and the devil meant for evil; God turned around for good. I was part of the plan of evil, because that is where my heart was that night.

I did not recognize that I'd been under the protection of the Lord that cold night in 1972 until after I got saved. How many people are in the same boat? God's dramatic protection is in operation in their lives and they do not have the spiritual awareness of God's protection. In protecting you, sometimes God will allow your enemies to experience death. The men that put Shadrach, Meshach, and AbedNego in the furnace were killed by the flame of that same fire. If you will wait on the Lord and trust in the Lord, He will promote you. The king promoted Shadrach, Meshach, and AbedNego because they refused to yield their bodies to worship any god except their own God! What a statement they made!

Believe in the Lord, and watch His dramatic protection. God is not selfish with His favor, if He did it for one He must do it for all. If you can find in the Bible where God protected anyone, then He must protect you. If today's Christians would behave like their ancient brothers, then evil would depart from their neighborhoods.

The faithfulness of these three Hebrew men also, I believe, helped King Nebuchadnezzar depart from sin and showing mercy to the poor. The King went from no personal relationship with God to having a ongoing personal relationship with God and recognizing God's kingship rather than his own authority. Nebuchadnezzar praised God and surrendered his kingship to God's ultimate rule. This is a lesson that each person could learn—we are kings in this life!

Look at the news of today—evil is on the rise. Confidence in the Lord and His goodness are missing today. God's merciful attitude is evident every place you look! Without the mercy of God, we would be up a creek without a paddle. If we could surrender our lives to God, recognizing His ultimate rule in everything we do, then His dramatic protection would be freely recognized.

My daughter found out about God's Dramatic Protection. While visiting her aunt in LA, she went to church and heard a message about Job. In the message, she heard that you needed to shake off the things and people that are holding you back from doing what God wanted to do in your life. She had a boyfriend who was unequally yoked to her. Her mother and I had prayed some time ago for all our children to line up with the Word of God.

My daughter found out, two days after returning from Los Angeles, that her boyfriend had being fooling around with someone else. She received a phone call from a friend who asked her what her boyfriend's name was. It turned out that at that time he was at this person's apartment, seeing another young lady.

God was watching my daughter's back! The Dramatic Protection of the Lord is in place to protect you from every scheme of the devil. My daughter had been set up good by the devil. His plan was to distract her from what God wants to do in her life. Her mother had warned her about this guy; that he was not what God wanted for her life, but she was disobedient and did not listen. God is an awesome God. An all-knowing God!

You might think you are getting away with something, but the God of the universe sees all and knows all. He protected my daughter's feelings from getting hurt any further. This guy was a tool from the devil, used to distract my daughter from her plan and purpose in life. This guy said all the right things and acted the right way! The devil comes as an angel of light.

God may allow something painful to continue to help you grow in your relationship with Him, but in the end, we win. My daughter did not feel hurt at all when she realized she had to break up with him. It was her decision, not our decision, and all is well. The Lord said He would not leave us or forsake us and He meant it. My only daughter has learned a valuable lesson in life about the deception of the devil. He comes to kill, steal, and destroy.

But do you know what he comes to kill, steal, and destroy? It is your relationship with God. If you do not have a relationship with God, you cannot hear from God like you should, therefore you get into ungodly relationships and affairs that God did not ordain for your life. If you are up to things in life that God did not ordain, then you are living outside of the will of God.

There are many people today who are not living in the will of God. Many marriages are broken because God did not ordain the people to be married to each other. Many business partnerships have gone broke, because God did not ordain the partners to be in business together. God is going to get the glory out of my daughter ex-boyfriend's life, because we serve an awesome God, a loving God, a mighty God, a faithful God, a caring God. He does not know that the devil is using him, just like many people in the world do not know that the devil is influencing them.

When I was a boy of twelve, I lived in Martinsburg, West Virginia with my grandmother Fannie Marks. There was a river that many of us kids liked to play near, but my grandmother warned me not to go there. I was not obedient, and my cousin George Johnson and I went anyway. He went north up the river and I went south up the river. As a kid, I did not always look where I was going. A part of the bank was soft and I fell into the river. The river was deep and I could not swim!

I remember going under when all of a sudden someone picked me up and put me on the bank. My cousin was not there, no one else was around either. When my cousin returned, he asked what had happen to me. I told him I fell into the river, but never told him that I could not swim, and certainly not that someone took me out of the river.

We were concerned about my grandmother finding out that I had fallen into the river, so we walked very slowly back home so that I could dry out. I did not tell anyone what had happened after I had fallen in. I was not sure what had happened. All that I knew was that I was going under, and all of a sudden I was picked up out of that water and placed on the bank. What I now know is that the dramatic protection of the Lord was in action that summer day in Martinsburg, West Virginia and a 12-year-old boy was saved from drowning.

Once I received the infilling of the Holy Spirit, I began to recognize incidents in my life that showed that God was so faithful. There is a song we sing at our church that is about looking back over our lives and seeing how God was faithful. This is the honest truth! When I look back over my life, I can see the dramatic protection of the Lord in my life. Daniel 9:9 is the perfect Scripture that talks about my life. To The Lord our God belong mercy and forgiveness, though we have rebelled against Him.

The Lord's mercy has covered me like a blanket and protected me. I should not be here today writing to you. If the devil had his way, I would have drowned in that river in West Virginia. After my Grandmother passed away, I went to live with my father and stepmother in my birthplace of New Castle, PA. One evening, we were getting ready to turn into our driveway, and a car came down the street at 100 miles per hour. It piled into us on the very side which I was sitting on. I did not receive one bruise or cut. I could have died in that car accident 36 years ago. Again, God was protecting me. The devil was trying to kill me so I could not write this book that would set the captives free. Both of these incidents occurred before I reached the age of adulthood.

Think about how many people have lost their lives before becoming adults or fulfilling the plan and purpose for their lives. God's plan and purpose are awesome ones that were laid out before the foundation of the earth. I had put myself into the wrong position that day at the river, and God still came through.

My grandmother had wisdom about rivers and what they can do to you. I was lacking in wisdom concerning rivers and what they can do to you. By being disobedient, I almost lost my life at an early age. God stepped in, and I believe changed the course of my life. This was not a dramatic illustration of the personal presence and protection of the Lord because of my testimony, but it was a dramatic illustration of the personal presence and protection of the Lord because of His love for mankind.

God had a plan and a purpose for my life and I had not begun to fulfill that plan and purpose on that hot summer day in West Virginia. I was raised in a Baptist Church and always loved going, but really did not have anyone ask me to accept Jesus as my Lord and Savior until I was stationed at Rickenbacker AFB, Ohio (Columbus, Ohio). I was 32 years-old before I asked Jesus into my heart. I never knew the power of God until I received the infilling of the Holy Spirit of God in July 1992 in Sacramento, California. God kept me until I received His Son.

I thought I was saved because I had gone to church all my life. How many of you are in this same boat? If you leave this earth today you will go to Hell because you have not accepted the Son of the living God as your personal Lord and Savior.

If you have not made a verbal confession according to Romans 10:9, you are not saved. I don't care if you have been in church 50 years, you are not saved according to the Word of truth (The Bible). I feel there are some of you reading this book that fall into that category. You have been around the church all your life, but have never made Jesus Lord and Savior of your life. If you are still alive and well, then start thanking the Lord for His dramatic protection and mercy. Do not take for granted the protection of the Lord. It has been, and always will be the Lord that protects you from dangers, or if you were in a car accident and lived to tell about it, it was the Lord that allowed you to walk free from injury.

Then King Nebuchadnezzar was astonished; and he rose in haste and spoke, saying to his counselors, "Did we not cast three men bound into the midst of the fire?" They answered and said to the king. "True, O king" (Dan. 3:24).

The dramatic protection of the Lord will cause people to be astonished. All of us if we think about it, have experienced the protection of God upon our lives. If we tell someone about our experiences, they will be astonished. What King Nebuchadnezzar found out is that we can be bound, but when the Lord shows up we will be loose as a goose. Nothing can stop the power of God from operating in your life when you are living right and lined up with the Word of God. No demon in Hell can stop the power of God from operating on behalf of a child of God that is in right standing with God.

I want to hammer this thought into your brain. There is no demon in Hell that can stop the power of God from operating on the behalf of a child of God that is in right standing with the Lord. God gave us a promise to stand on. He said, I will never leave you or forsake you (Josh. 1:5). Forsake means to abandon. God has given us a promise that He will not abandon us. If any one tells me that they won't leave or abandon me, I want it to be the God of Abraham, Jacob, and Isaac. Leave means to let go. Again, God has promised us He will not let go of us. He holds us in the palm of His hands! Since God will not abandon or let go of us, we should be thanking Him for His dramatic protection every day of our lives.

Each day is not promised to us. It is by the dramatic protection of the Lord and His mercy that we see another day. We can not take for granted the dramatic protection of the Lord every. He knows each hair on your head. God, help us to understand that You know everything about us. The Word says He knew us when we were formed in our mother's womb. You notice it does not say while we were in our Mother's womb, but when we were formed in our mother's womb. He (God) formed us in our Mother's womb. I know I am going to lose some of you, but the actual Father of each person on this earth is God. So as a good Father, why wouldn't He want to protect His worthy children (saved) and unworthy children (unsaved)?

The Bible says that in the beginning, God made man and woman. God put into Adam His reproductive system and He put into Eve His reproductive system. The first children from Adam and Eve came as a result of what God deposited into Adam and Eve; which was He. From that first seed, every man and woman have come forth. But the original seed came from God and is still producing today. Each time a baby is born into this world that seed from God is producing. If you don't think of reproduction like that, then ask God for the revelation. The Word says we have not, because we ask not. You might say the unsaved are not the children of God. Well then, why does God care so much for the unsaved to know him?

Look for a moment at the story of the prodigal son (Luke 15:11-32). One son was obedient and worked the fields, while the other son (the youngest), went into a strange land and spent all his money. He was disobedient. The father still loved him even though he spent all His money. God still loves the unsaved child.

The Word is very clear, God so loved the world that He gave His only begotten Son (John 3:16). God is always trying to get you to come home to Him, and the devil is always trying to get you to stay away from home.

The further away from God you are, the less dramatic protection of the Lord you experience. The devil's job is to get you out of the dramatic protection of the Lord. He can never accomplish that feat, but your experience level will not be as high as it could be. The further you are from the presence of God, the less your experience level of the dramatic protection of the Lord will be. Some people's experience level of the dramatic protection of the Lord is not very much, while other people's experience level of the dramatic protection of the Lord is 10 times greater then the fiery furnace of Daniel. That means the devil can not get near you, because of the dramatic protection of the Lord. I believe this protection only comes through consistent fellowship with the Lord. Don't get me wrong, God will protect all; but some people are protected from even rats in their home! That may not be a big deal that's my point: the smallest thing in our life is a big thing to God. He never lets us out of His sight.

The dramatic protection of the Lord can come in all forms. He can protect you from all the little distractions at church that are trying to steal the Word from you. The Word says that Satan comes immediately to steal the Word. The protection of the Lord will cause that distraction to go from you so that the Word of God will not be stolen from you. You may have not thought of the dramatic protection of the Lord in this way; but if the Word is stolen from you, you have nothing to stand on; just what the devil wants. No Word in; no Word out. Without your weapon (the Word) you have no defense against the devil, therefore, he can run a touchdown against you and score at will. The Word of God is a defense as well as a offense weapon against the devil. Without the dramatic protection of the Lord, the Word would be stolen from you each time it is preached to you.

How do you stop the devil from stealing from you? God got that taken care of too. When you authorize the Holy Spirit of God to teach you, and you yield yourself to the Holy Spirit; you stop the devil from stealing the Word from you. The Word says the Holy Spirit will teach you all truth. He will not let the devil steal from you.

How do you authorize the Holy Spirit to teach you? By saying it with your mouth and yielding to the Holy Spirit. When you decrease; the Holy Spirit can increase. You can say, "I decrease and you Holy Spirit increase." When those words are spoken; you will hear things from the Word of God that you never understood before. Not only will you understand the Word of God, but also you will see the dramatic protection of the Lord like never before. God is in everything in your life, but you will finally understand it like never before.

I said the Holy Spirit would not let the devil steal from you, but you might let the devil steal from you. God will not stop you, but will do all He can in His power to warn you. It is up to you to be obedient! If you are obedient to the Holy Spirit you will experience the dramatic protection of the Lord just like the three Hebrew young men did in the fiery furnace. They called upon something else also: courage. What does courage have to do with the dramatic protection of the Lord?

Without courage in the excellent name of Jesus and the Father God, the three Hebrew young men would have been lunch meat on the king's table. They did not back down on their stand that there is only one God worth serving and worshipping. Today we accept all kinds of gods instead of recognizing that there is only one God and that is the living God of Abraham, Jacob, and Isaac.

Courage will bring the dramatic protection of the Lord to your defense. God cannot sit back and watch when you demonstrate the kind of courage that the three Hebrew young men demonstrated in the fiery furnace. There is happiness for those whose help or dramatic protection is the Lord.

Do not put your trust in princes. Nor in man, in whom there is no help. His spirit departs, he returns to his earth; In that very day his Plans perish. Happy is he who has the God of Jacob for his help, Whose hope is in the Lord his God (Ps.146: 35).

Happy is he whose dramatic protection comes from the Lord and not from man, in whom there is no help or protection. Man cannot protect you; only God can protect you. There is a false-trust alive in the world today. Many people have installed in their homes alarm systems to protect them. This is a false trust; if someone broke into your home only the dramatic protection of the Lord could protect you. You could shoot the person, but you will probably go on trail for shooting the person.

If the dramatic protection of the Lord is in operation; then the person can be stopped and detained by the Lord until the police arrive. Most Christians act as if the Lord is dead, but the Word says Jesus rose from the dead and is seated at the right hand of the Father in Heaven.

One of the present-day ministries of Jesus is to intercede for us. If Jesus is interceding for us; then He is not dead, but alive! When Jesus walked the earth, His ministry was teaching, preaching, and healing. He left the teaching, preaching, and healing in our hands when He returned to Heaven. But He did not stop His ministry; He relocated where He is today.

Protection is one of the present-day ministries of the Lord. The devil and his crowd know that Jesus is alive, but most of God's children do not believe that Jesus is alive. They say they do; but their actions do not indicate they believe He is alive. They do not act on their faith, and without faith it is impossible to please God. Faith is an action word! If you are not calling on the dramatic protection of the Lord by faith, then you are not pleasing God and not operating in faith.

Believe, Believe, Believe, that Jesus Christ the Son of the living God is alive and He will do what He says He will do. Jesus is the same yesterday, today, and forever more! Since Jesus is in Heaven; He is not on earth to protect us like He did the first disciples; but His spiritual dramatic protection is available to each believer that will reach out by faith and grab it.

Everything we obtain from God must come through the arena of faith. Again, without faith it is impossible to please God. God has made it easy; He has given us His faith to operate with. If we will operate with His faith; giving His faith back to Him; we will be pleasing Him. Can you see how God makes it so easy for you to please Him; but man makes it so hard to please Him?

Why do we not use our faith to grab the dramatic protection of the Lord? One reason is the lack of understanding regarding our right to use the Name of Jesus! This lack of understanding will hold us in bondage and will give us a sense of weakness. But when we know that we know that we know what that Name will do, we can take our rightful position of authority over Satan and enjoy victory. We should know that Jesus' Name has authority and power on the earth today and that His Name belongs to us.

Most of the Body of Christ does not understand what I just said: that the Name of Jesus belongs to us and carries authority and power on the earth today. Most have not taken their rightful position of authority over Satan. Jesus died to give you dramatic protection.

Another reason why we do not use our faith to grab the dramatic protection of the Lord is our lack of understanding about acting on the Word. We should stop trying to make God's Word work, and start acting on the Word. If we know that the Word is true and if we act as though it is true, it becomes a reality in our lives.

Our Pastor acted upon the Word instead of trying to believe when he brought the church that is now our Chapel, without any money, but by faith he purchased a 3 million dollar building for $825,000. He had only fifty people in his congregation at that point. He acted like The Word is true.

Faith calls forth those things that are not into existence! In the spiritual bank, each of us has an account of dramatic protection. We must reach into the Spirit and call forth our dramatic protection of the Lord into existence. Your account of dramatic protection may be full because you have not been using it. Some of you have never used your dramatic protection account. Some of you have never called upon the angels of the Lord to help you in any form. I hope you will start to call upon your dramatic protection account. It is yours!

Why do you refuse to use it? The Lord opened up your account at Calvary over 2000 years ago, and He is waiting for your participation. As your faith grows, you begin to possess rights in Christ. You begin to take hold of what belongs to you in Christ. You begin to take hold of things that you only hoped for before.

You hoped for protection before, but now, by faith, you have it. If you are sick, you need to confess, "By His stripes I am healed!" You can't confess that and confess that you are still sick at the same time! If you say you are still sick, then you are perhaps agreeing that the Word is still true, but you haven't acted upon it and received it for yourself in your own life. If you say, "By His stripes I am healed, and, therefore, I'm not sick," then you are acting upon the Word.

You can reach that place of walking in divine health by acting upon God's Word. The dramatic protection of the Lord is part of the package of salvation. The Hebrew and Greek words for salvation imply the ideas of deliverance, safety, preservation, healing, and soundness. We must believe the Word of God! Safety and protection are the same thing. If God protected three young Hebrew men who were not born again, and who were under the old covenant how much more will he protect His children who are under a new and better covenant?

Jesus is coming again, whether we believe it or not. He is coming because the Word says so. The resurrection is going to take place whether we have faith or not. Whether we believe in it or not, it is still going to take place. The rapture is going to take place whether we believe in it or not. And loved ones and friends who are Christians, who have died and left this world and have gone to Heaven are there, regardless of what we believe about it. And they will return with Jesus when He comes back.

God does not play favorites. He plays the game of life by faith. To get the dramatic protection of the Lord operating in your life you must claim it now. Faith is now! Someone said, "I believe God is going to heal me." But that isn't faith. That's hope. Anything that points to the future or looks to the future is hope. It is not faith because faith is now.

Faith says, "It is mine. I have it now." Hope says, "I'll get it sometime." But as long as you live only in hope and not in faith, whatever it is you are desiring may never materialize—it could never come into being. But the moment you start believing and acting like God's Word is so, your faith will work for you.

You cannot believe beyond actual knowledge. You must know what the Word says. You must say to the Lord, "Lord, I believe I receive the dramatic protection from my spiritual account now," that's when your faith is working for you. Why do we need the dramatic protection of the Lord? Because Satan, though he has only temporary influence, he has a counterfeit plan—a crafty imitation of the real.

We must not forget that Satan is exceedingly clever. When he fell in his rebellion, he did not lose the gifts and genius God put into him. He is a master deceiver.

Here are five ways Satan, from his dark kingdom counterfeits, or falsely imitates, everything God has done: (1) Satan offers those who follow him a counterfeit family. (2) Satan has created a counterfeit gospel. (3) Satan also has established counterfeit ministers. (4) Satan offers a counterfeit righteousness. (5) Satan seeks his own counterfeit worship.

We are in a fierce battle with the Enemy of our souls. Spiritual warfare is a biblical reality. It occurs whether we acknowledge it or not. Satan doesn't need our assent to attack us. If we are not on guard, wearing our spiritual armor and equipped with the tools of biblical warfare, he will try to rip our lives apart.

Satan's kingdom is a structured organization of supernatural evil. Originally, it was part of Christ's perfect creation and under His authority. Scripture plainly reveals that the Lord Jesus Christ created those in Satan's kingdom. As the Creator, He holds the kingdom of darkness answerable to Him. As a structured kingdom, the throne of darkness is still subservient to Christ. Thus, in Christ's power, we can stand against the devil's schemes. For sovereign purposes known only to God, the kingdom of darkness is allowed to continue to rebel and function until God's perfect time comes to judge Satan and his host. At that moment, God will cast all the fallen spiritual beings into the lake of fire prepared for them.

Satan, however, will seek to distract us from our spiritual regeneration through the Spirit by degeneration in our flesh. His attacks will center on our body appetites (physical), our desires (emotional), and our thoughts and beliefs (intellectual and spiritual). The Lord has given His Holy Spirit as dramatic protection against the works of Satan. He is a defeated and spoiled foe! Remember that when Satan comes your way. The dramatic protection of the Lord will carry you to victory in every area of your life if you will let Him.

Chapter Twelve

What the Blood of Jesus Christ Says to You

Do you know that the blood of Jesus speaks to us? The Bible says it does (Heb. 12:22-24). There are eight ways the blood of Jesus Christ speaks to us:

- You are justified.
- You are redeemed.
- You have peace.
- You are God's property.
- You have eternal salvation.
- You are clean.
- You are washed.
- You have victory.

Romans 5:9 says, Being now justified by his blood, we shall be saved from wrath through him.

Justified is a term that not many people understand. It means the same as acquitted, declared innocent, not guilty. When you go into a court of law, a jury hears all the evidence, and they ponder that evidence, and come back with a verdict to the judge. The verdict will be either guilty or not guilty. That is what happened at Calvary.

There, the greatest Court session in history was held for the human race. The Judge was our Father; the Lawyer was our Savior, the Lord Jesus Christ. The jury brought in the verdict for all that accept Jesus into their hearts—not guilty! We have been saved, through Jesus Christ, from the wrath of God that will come upon the world. Those who accept Jesus into their hearts have been acquitted from the curse that was placed on mankind at the fall of Adam, because of the death of Jesus.

All of mankind was sentenced to eternal death, but Jesus died in our place. His blood spoke in The Heavenly Court and said "They are justified." We received a free gift from God that great day at Calvary. Romans 6:23 says, The wages of sin is death; but the gift of God is eternal life through Jesus Christ our Lord.

In order to be justified you must Believe, Believe, Believe. It will not do you any good just to know that the blood of Jesus Christ speaks for you—you must believe without doubting that the blood of Jesus Christ speaks for you. Your eternal well-being is depending on what you believe. The blood of Jesus Christ has justified you! You must think like God to have what God has given you. The Word says the Lamb of God was slain for the world. If you slay any animal you will have blood being spilled. The Lamb of God is Jesus Christ who was slain on Calvary for the sin of the world. What sin was Jesus slain for? The sin that gets mankind into all kinds of trouble disobedience! Adam was disobedient to God which open the door for all kinds of sin to follow. If mankind would be obedient then God would be happy with mankind.

It was by one man's (Adam) disobedience that death entered into the world and it was by one man's (Jesus) obedience that life entered into the world. What death are we talking about? Eternal death or separation from God! What life are we talking about? Eternal life or being with God? Which one would you choose?

Every person born comes into this world under the curse of Adam. But, thanks God, you do not have to stay under the curse. God made a way for you to escape through Jesus Christ. That is the reason Satan fights so hard to keep you captive. God has put before you the greatest escape artist— Jesus Christ. This world does not understand that the border to freedom is just a few feet away. What a shame! Jesus is your freedom maker.

After the civil war, slaves were free to go their own way, but many of them stayed and helped the same people who had treated them so badly, not realizing they could go on and prosper in life. This is the same thing that is taking place in mankind today. Jesus already purchased freedom for all of mankind and only about three fourth of mankind has taken part in this purchase plan. There are six billion people upon this earth, and only three-fourths of them know of the gift of God—salvation. The border to freedom is in giving your life over to Jesus and letting the Holy Spirit of God control your life. The Creator of life is God! Since He is the Creator; why is the creation trying to tell the Creator how they should run their lives? We have been justified by the Blood of the Lamb. The Creator's blood was given to us to bring us back in fellowship with Him. This is love!

If you are reading this book and you are a Christian or nonChristian, you should be thanking God for His love. The Bible says the Word was God, and the Word was made flesh and dwelt among the people—Jesus. Jesus was born of a virgin and grew to take upon His shoulders the sin of the world. If you have any thoughtfulness in you then you can see what love God has for mankind. He took Himself and gave Himself so that mankind did not have to be separated from Him. Jesus is God; The Holy Spirit is God, and God The Father is God. God the Father, the Son, and the Holy Spirit!

When we were justified, the Father judged the Son, who was innocent for the guilt of mankind. You see mankind was guilty, but Jesus took on our guilt as a scapegoat for mankind. The road to freedom is narrow, but well traveled. If you are traveling on a road where there is a narrow bridge, you will always see a sign to warn you. The sign that the Father has given mankind to warn them is the Bible (The Word of God).

Every sign of the bridge of life being narrow is recorded in the Bible. People either don't see the sign, overlook the sign, don't understand the sign, or don't care about the sign. People are having accidents on life's narrow bridge. One accident in life will cause others to have accidents also. Can you see the seriousness of looking, understanding, and caring about the warning signs of the Bible? These signs are responsible for you getting eternal life and not eternal death. The bridge of life is very, very narrow, yet with the guidance of the Holy Spirit, the bridge of life is very, very broad.

Jesus had two roles at Calvary—Lawyer and Prisoner. As Lawyer, He defended us, and still does in His present day ministry. As Prisoner, He took our place, commended for the curse placed upon mankind by God the Father. The blood of Jesus says we have been redeemed from the curse of the law. The blood that was sprinkled in The High Court of Heaven gives us a right to be free from miseries, poverty, pain, sickness, and diseases, which sin, brought into this world. You have victory over these curses in the Name of Jesus, in whom we have redemption through His Blood.

When people realized that because of The blood of Jesus sickness has got to go, poverty must take a hike, miseries are not welcome, and pain has got to leave; then, and only then, will they walk in the fullness of God.

The blood of Jesus gives you victory in every area of your life. Jesus said He came not only to give you life, but abundant life. When you apply the blood of Jesus to every area of your life, you walk in abundant life. We have been washed in the blood of Jesus. Every sin we've ever committed has been washed away from us and forgotten because of the blood of Jesus. I am not making any of this up. Do you believe the Bible or not? Hebrews12:22-24 tells us that the blood of Jesus speaks to us.

When Mary saw Jesus, and He told her not to touch Him (John 20:17). He said that He had not yet ascended to His Father. Later, He told the disciples to touch and feel Him. The Blood had to be Holy. I know this is hard to understand, but I believe that Jesus left earth and went to Heaven to present His Blood to redeem mankind, then returned to earth, walked on the earth for 40 days and left for Heaven, to remain there until His enemy is made His footstool.

The Bible does not say that Jesus left earth twice, but ladies and gentlemen, I wonder, how did His Blood get to Heaven, if Jesus was not the one who presented His Blood to the Father for the redemption of man? This is a subject that some of you will not agree with me on, It is my opinion that the redemption of man could not wait 40 days and 40 nights until He instructed His disciples.

I believe that the fulfillment of the redemption of man took place immediately after Jesus rose from the dead. Again, the Bible does not record that, but it is my opinion. Mary, I believe, caught Jesus on His way to make the down payment with His Blood for man and that is why He told her not to touch Him yet.

The blood of Jesus says we have been purchased back from the evil one. He no longer as any legal right to us. But like the slaves during the Civil War, who did not know that legally they had been set free two years prior to their actual release, most people do not know that they have been set free. They must believe that God raised Jesus from the dead and make a confession that Jesus rules their lives and not themselves and they will be set free.

Satan is like the Southern slave owners who did not let the slaves know that they were free. Freedom for mankind was purchased by the blood of Jesus some 2000 years ago, but you must believe to receive your freedom. Satan keeps most people in bondage because they do not believe in Jesus. If people would just check out the Word of God they would find out that they are free. God says that whoever seeks Him will find Him. There is an ongoing war (spiritual) that a billion people are engaged in.

Why is it that the Book given by the Most High God is not read or understood? Because the devil's job is to keep you from either reading the Bible or if you read the Bible not understanding it. God gave us His Holy Spirit to make the Word of God plan to us. But many of us read the Bible each and every day without the assistance of the Holy Spirit. Without the Holy Spirit's assistance we get either wrong guidance or direction from the Word.

The blood of Jesus Christ says you are free from the law of sin and death. Why are many people not free? The reason is unbelief. If you don't believe, you can't receive. The blood of Jesus the Anointed One and His anointing freed you from the law of sin and death some 2000 years ago, but like the slaves in the Civil War, you don't know that you are free, and most people do not even have the documents (The Bible) in their homes that tell them that they are free.

The ones who have the document are not reading it to obtain information about their freedom. They accept what the slave-master (the devil) says. All of what the blood of Jesus says is important, but if there is one thing that is of utmost importance it is that you are free from the law of sin and death. Sin separates you from God just as well as death separates you from God.

In this world, there are a lot of people who do not know that they are under the cruse of sin and death. To put it mildly they are separated from God, unable to hear clearly the directions of God for their life. The blood of Jesus did away with this separation from God!

God gives us a command: to seek after His Kingdom and His Righteousness. When we make this our target, the blood of Jesus takes us away from everything that is sin to God and takes us toward everything that is good to God. Why can the blood of Jesus do this? It has already happen 2000 years ago. We are still in the Church Age, so what Jesus accomplished on the cross some 2000 years ago, is currently just as powerful as ever.

Chapter Thirteen

Who is Blessed and Who is Cursed?

Thus says the Lord. "Cursed is the man who trusts in man. And makes flesh His strength, Whose heart departs from the Lord. For he shall be like a shrub in the desert, And shall not see when good comes, but shall inhabit the parched places in the wilderness, In a salt land which is not inhabited. Blessed is the man who trusts in the Lord. And whose hope is the Lord. For he shall be like a tree planted by the waters, Which spreads out its roots by the river, And will not fear when heat comes; but its leaf will be green, and will not be anxious in the year of drought. Nor will cease from yielding fruit."

The heart is deceitful above all things, And desperately wicked: Who can know it? "I, the Lord, search the heart, I test the mind. Even to give every man according to his ways, According to the fruit of his doings" (Jer. 17:5-10).

Believing the Word of God is profitable to you. Who does God say is blessed and who does He say is cursed? The man or woman who puts his or her trust in man instead of the Lord is under a curse. The Merriam Webster's Collegiate Dictionary says that a curse is a cause of great harm or misfortune.

If you have had misfortune come upon you, stop and think for a moment. Why do these things happen to you? The answer probably lies in Jeremiah 17:5-10. Maybe you have knowingly, or perhaps unknowingly, put your trust in man and not the Lord. Scripture does not discriminate: you can be a Christian or a non-Christian and have your trust in man and not the Lord. Most likely, if you are not a Christian you do not have your trust in the Lord anyway.

Before you trust someone, you must be in a relationship with him or her. A non-Christian is not in a relationship with the Lord. This can apply to the ungodly man or the godly man who is operating in unbelief. Either one's relationship with the Lord is damaged.

Who else does the Lord say is cursed? A man or woman who makes the flesh their strength. In other words, trying to make things happen instead of depending on the Lord to make things happen for you. Another way of saying that you have made the flesh your strength is that you have allowed yourself to take the place of God.

Remember the story of the Garden of Eden? The devil put it into Eve's mind that when she ate of the fruit, she would become like God. Mankind to this day is still trying to be god over their selves. What is so sad about the incident in the Garden of Eden is that we are already made in the likeness of God. Eve was already what she was trying to become.

So what was the big deal? It was, and is today—disobedience. We cannot make anything happen, and God can make everything happen! The ability to know that you are like God was temporary taken from man. We must now be born again to know that we know that we know; we are made in the image of God.

When you put your strength in the flesh, you are putting your trust in the powerless strength of man. Not only are you powerless, but you are cursed also. You could say that double, double trouble is upon you. Nothing you do will work!

You may have heard of people who win the lottery and then within the next year or two, end up flat broke. Have you ever ask yourself the question why? The Bible can answer that question: Cursed is the man or woman who puts their trust in man and not in God.

The lottery is a form of gambling; only it's legalized gambling. When you gamble, your are putting your trust in someone other then God. Many Christians are playing the lottery not knowing that it's not a blessing from God, but a curse. In Jeremiah 17:5 it says, Cursed is the man who trusts in man.

So let me ask you a question. Is your trust in God, or in man when you play the lottery? You may know Christians who have won the lottery. I do too, but does that make it right? We are in the last days, right things are being called wrong and wrong things are being called right.

For he shall be like a shrub in the desert, and shall not see when good comes, but shall inhabit the parched places in the wilderness, in a salt land which is not inhabited (Jer. 17:6).

Have you seen a shrub in the desert? It's not able to grow to its full potential. Your growth in life will not come to fulfillment. God will curse every area of your life! Look at the world today; people are making more money then they ever made in the past and are in more debt then they ever where in the past. Why? They are blinded to the good that comes from the Lord. So like that shrub in the desert, people are dry when it comes to fulfilling the potential that God placed into their lives. They are not satisfied with life.

Just recently, a basketball player turned down a 90 million dollar contract, and then a 70 million dollar contract to play in the city were just four years ago he said he would love to play in. Why? He is like that shrub in the desert. The shrub in the desert is not happy because it is out of place. Someone who is trusting in man and not in God is out of place. One of the commandments of God is You shall have no other gods before Me (Exod. 20:3). Trusting in man makes a god out of man and places him before God Himself.

Do you see now why you are cursed if you put your trust in man or make flesh your strength? You have violated one of the Ten Commandments given to Moses! We do not talk much about the Ten Commandments, but they are still enforced today. Since God is the same today, yesterday, and forevermore, His Word is still effective. If you play the lottery, you are putting a god before God Himself. He is to provide all our needs!

The reason so much is looked at today as right when it's actually wrong, and so much is counted wrong when it's actually right is because we do not know the instructions of the Bible.

The reading or posting of the Ten Commandments has been taken out of the schools—a trick of the devil! If you want a group of people to learn something, one of the ways to help them learn is to keep it before them. If you want this same group of people to unlearn something one of the ways to help them unlearn is to keep it away from them. You cannot learn to do something if you are not taught. By saying The Ten Commandments before each day started you were being taught to obey them. See no one had to tell you to obey them; you knew to obey them. If you stole something you were convicted, not because of the theft, but because you broke one of The Ten Commandments. That conviction is not evident in society today. The person who convinced the Supreme Court that The Ten Commandments violated the Constitution was an agent of the devil.

What is sad is that Christians sat and let one person place a whole nation (United States of America) under the curse mentioned in Jeremiah. The very first thing mentioned comes to mind. Cursed is the man who trusts in man. This country was founded on the Word of God. Our money says In God We Trust! When The Ten Commandments were not allowed to be read in the public schools this country went from trusting in God to trusting in man.

What answer can you give any educated man or woman who questions the moral decline of our country over the last 38 years? It's very plain, we have taken our trust from God and placed it in man. Just stop and think. Once this country was the number one car manufacturers in the world. Now, the United States of America is catching up with the Third World countries in the amount of homeless people we have. We have gone away from God and have gone to man. We have more people that put their trust in the lottery than the Almighty God.

The Word of God says you will be like a shrub in a desert when you put your trust in man. What is a desert? A desert is a tract incapable of supporting any considerable population without an artificial water supply. God is saying you are like a shrub, which needs a water supply to fully grow is placed into a desert. This is man who trusts in man and not in God for the supply of life.

Even if you win the lottery, you still are incapable of receiving the true blessings of Christ in your life. Blessings that, no matter what happens, will keep coming and coming. Blessings may someday come your way, but you will not be walking in the full blessings that God has to offer to His children who are walking on course with His Word.

Some folks recently purchased tickets in the lottery which was 61 million—and they won—9 dollars. They got back a reward, but not the full reward they could have gotten. Now they are trying again—Satan's trap was laid and they took the bait.

But seek first the Kingdom of God and His righteousness, and all these things shall be added to you (Matt. 6:33).

What "things" are God talking about—what we eat, what we drink, and what we wear. Life's essentials! We do not have to worry about any need in life, if we will just do what God's Word says to do. If you are obedient you will eat the fat of the land. Most Christians have not read Jeremiah 17:5-10 in their entire Christian life.

As any father, God tells us what to do and what not to do. He spells out what will happen if we don't do what He tells us, and spells out what will happen if we do what He tells us to do. We must learn the will of God to get anything from Him. God is a loving Father who cares so much about His children that He gave His only Son. If your heart departs from Him, no good will come to you. God tells you this fact.

Most parents care more about their own children than they do about the next door neighbor's children. The next door neighbor cares about their children, but not as much about the your children. That is what happens if God's children start playing with the devil; the devil doesn't care about you. I take that back, he does care about you—he hates you! Child of God, get this into your spirit—he hates you.

He only plays with you to get next to your Daddy (God the Father). The Father cannot and will not bless unrighteousness. It goes against His very nature, but lines squarely up with the nature of the devil. He blesses the unrighteous each and everyday. Satan's power was not taken from him when he fell from Heaven. God's power is greater, but Satan's power was not taken from him. We have power in Christ to defeat the devil who is already a defeated and spoiled foe.

When you see sinners getting rich, God says not to envy them. The playing field for the sinner is just for a moment, but the playing field for the born again believer is forever. You can jump for joy that you are not going to Hell, but also take every opportunity to lead someone to Christ out of the kingdom of darkness. Brothers and Sisters who do not know the truth can be lead to the truth by you. Always be on the alert to help someone understand and find the truth—either to salvation or out of bondage.

If you are cursed, good can be all around you and you cannot see it. I did not write any of the Bible, the Holy Spirit of God through faithful men wrote the Bible. So if you have a problem with what I said that good can be all around you an you would not see it, then take it up with God.

God says when you are trusting in man, good will come to you, but you will not see it. The Word of God speaks for itself. How many people do you know that have passed up what you know to be a golden opportunity in life? You knew it was a once-in-a-lifetime opportunity, but the person could not see it. What is that? Just what God said would happen—they shall not see when good comes. Good will come, but the person will be blinded to see what is happening.

Who is blinding them and why? The answer to that question is simple—the devil, and because he hates you. If you see good coming; it brings glory to God and Satan wants the glory for himself. God tells you that good will come, not that it might come, but that it will come. If you have put your trust in man instead of God, now is the time to put your trust back in the loving hands of God, so when good comes you can see it coming and take advantage of all the blessings of God. Our Father can't make it any more plain.

If you put your trust in man you will inhabit the parched places in the wilderness and not the green places in the garden. Those who have put their trust in man live in the wilderness of life. Stop an think about that for a moment! To many people, the wilderness of life is the place they call home. Why are they there? Because they have put their trust in man and now according to the Word of God which cannot return void to Him they are cursed. As any loving Father, God gives them a way out of their position in life.

Trust! Believe on Jesus, believe God, and believe His Word. God's Word is here to stay, but the only thing keeping people in the land of the cursed is not believing or knowing the Word. God's Word says that the heart (the inner self, which thinks, feels, and acts) is deceitful above all things. This is the real you. Why is it deceitful? Because we took on the nature of the devil after the fall of Adam. Before Adam fell, he had the nature of God, after he fell, he acquired the nature of the devil.

Each person born into this world comes into the world with this nature! It is a deceitful nature that stays with a person until they accept Jesus as their Lord and Savior, then we are born again or our nature is recreated in Christ Jesus. If you are truly recreated, you are incapable of sinning and sinning. The nature of God will convict you and bring about repentance. If you are capable of sinning without any conviction, then I wonder about your true salvation. Something is wrong if you do not come under conviction—not commendation, but conviction.

Commendation takes you from God and conviction takes you to God. Commendation is from the devil and conviction is from God. It you are in the wilderness of life and do not know why, check yourself out and see if you have allowed yourself to trust in man rather than trusting in God. Study the Word of God to see if you are doing the Will of God. You can, out of your own ignorance, be labeled an ungodly or unbelieving man. Do not be caught in that label. Curses are not the perfect will of God for your life. God paid a heavy price for you.

Please, I beg you! Examine yourself and see if you have allowed any area of your life to come under the trust of man and not under the trust of God. The textbook for this examination is the Bible. Do not use any other textbook for this examination. The final exam is too important of a test. It's eternal life or eternal death. God gives you the choice and provides the open book for you to study. Many of His children are too lazy to study and to thereby show themselves approved unto Him, a workman that needs not to be ashamed. I am focussing in depth on curses because it too important a subject to leave hanging in the wind. Most of the world does not realize that we are living in a world that has been cursed by the Almighty God.

God is such a loving God that He does not want anyone to remain in a cursed land. He wants you in the land of milk and honey, but the only way that you are going to go in and kill the giants is buy putting your trust in the Lord and not in man. Who is blessed? A born again person who trust in the Lord. Who is cursed? Any person who trust in man.

I believe God is still trying to reach us. That is why He put it upon my heart to write this book. He wants you to know who is blessed and who is cursed. He is not a respecter of person, if He has done it for one, He will do it for another. Joseph was blessed in a country that was not his own, because he trusted in the Lord. Supernatural favor was upon his life because he trusted in the Lord. Supernatural favor can be upon you because you trust in the Lord. Do you know what supernatural favor is? The Bible definition for blessed is the object of God's favor. How do you get to be blessed or the object of God's favors?

The only way that you can jump into this place is by being obedient to God's Word, which is the Will of God. The answer for how you can walk day by day in the blessings of God, as well as who is blessed is found in the examination book called the Bible.

If you have ever played a sport, you know that each sport has what is called a playbook. In order to play for that team, you must learn the playback for that team. God put out a playbook that never changes (The Bible) and for each member of the Body of Christ it is required learning in order to play in the field of Christian living.

If you will start today studying the Word to show yourself approved unto God, the field of life will become easier for you. Because you will not lean upon your own self, but will learn to lean upon the Lord for each and every decision in life.

Who is cursed? Those who lean upon their own self or put their trust in others instead of the Lord. Why would you take your Ford to a Buick dealership to get it fixed? Why do you trust your life, which is more important to someone other then God? The body of man was made by God, bears God's image and is wonderfully made—by God. Trust in the Creator, not the creation.

If you are blessed, then stay that way. If you have stumbled into the land of the cursed, there is a way out. Start putting all of your trust in the Lord. He came to not only give you life, but abundant life.

Do you know someone who is operating under the curse? Then you know someone who is out of the will of God. He or she are not partaking in the blessings of God, but are in the curses of God. God loves us so much because He is a holy God, He must curse those who do not follow His laws.

Our Pastor and two other Pastors were involved in an accident in our town, and each walked away without any broken bones. I would say that they are truly blessed. God watched over their lives. God says Touch not my anointed. Do my prophets no harm (1 Chron. 16:22).

This country which was founded on the Word of God needs to get back to the roots. Our money says In God We Trust. Can we The United States of America say that we trust in God? I think not. We have over 22 trillion dollars in this country, and yet in each major city you go to, you see homeless people. What is up? It does not take a rocket scientist to figure out the answer: We have gone away from worshipping and serving God as a country.

We do have Christians in America, but we can be called a pagan country. A pagan country is one where the majority are not serving God. We have more people serving false gods then serving the living God. You must recognize the seriousness of the situation. We have gone from a God-fearing country to a pagan country.

We have generations of kids who have no idea who God is or who Jesus Christ is. Because our forefathers sowed a great harvest when this country was formed, we are living off the benefits of their sowing, but each year more and more ungodliness settles into The United States of America.

Once we had the automobile trade sowed up, and then, when we sent God out of the schools, our automobile trade died. Japan now leads us, where before we led Japan in automobile trade. It is not because the Japanese know how to make cars better. It is because this country took the presence of God out of it.

Think were we would be as a country if three-fourths of The United States of America was serving God. The blessings this country enjoys today is because of the sowing of our forefathers. If we do not turn around, the homeless will keep on increasing. Yes, we are a blessed country, but we are not walking in the full blessings of God upon this country.

The full blessings of God will cause no one to be unemployed in this country. Food and housing for all. When Israel came out of Egypt there were over 3 million people, and the Bible says none were feeble. God's blessings were upon Israel while they were in Egypt and will be upon those who serve Him with all their heart, all their mind, and all their soul.

Read the Bible—all of Israel came out of Egypt with gold and silver belonging to the Egyptians. Israel may have been cursed while they were salves of Egypt, but when God freed them, they came out of Egypt fully blessed. God is a covenant-keeping God; He is waiting to bless all that will put their trust in Him. There is only one way to Him, and that is thorough the Lord Jesus.

You can only know the Father thorough the Son. God wants to bless His people, but most of His people operate under the curse and not under the blessings. He gave us His instructions (The Bible) and now it is up to us to follow His instructions if we are to receive those blessings.

You must get the Word of God inside of you, because what is on the inside will produce what is on the outside. You must know God, not just know of God. A personal relationship with the Lord is a must to receiving the blessings of God. That personal relationship is your pass into the land of honey (blessings). There is a giant in the land who does not want you to come into the blessings and he is doing all he can to make sure the majority of God's children do not come into their blessings.

What are their blessing? The gift of God's grace. What are some of the blessings of God? They are prosperity (Mal. 3:10-12), food and clothing (Matt. 6:26, 30-33) and longevity (Ex. 20:12). Have you lived over 70 years, or know of someone who has lived over 70 years? You can say that he or she is blessed. They have received the gift of God's grace.

Do you know someone who is rich and living a holy life for God? He or she is also blessed and have received the gift of God's grace. God wants you to have money, He does not want money to have you. The love of money is the root of all evil, not having money (1 Tim. 6:10). You can have two pennies to your name and still love money. You are to be a good steward of the money God allows you to have.

The story of the rich young ruler tells us that money can have you (Luke 18:18-25). God is not to take second place to anyone or anything. He is to be first place in your life! What is the definition of curse? It is a violent expression of evil upon others. If you are cursed, the gift of God's grace will not come looking for you. The only thing you will find is a violent expression of evil upon you. Get this definition in your heart we are not just talking about evil coming upon you, but a violent expression of evil coming upon you. You do not stand a chance in life if you are operating under the curse.

Two ways that the curse can be pronounced upon you are rebelliousness (2 Sam. 16:58) and disobedience (Deut. 28:15-45). Both of these ways operate in the earth today in the lives of men and women both Christians and non-Christians. The majority of people on the earth today can claim one or both of these titles. The fruit of the curse comes from disobedience, but the manifestation comes in the form of rebellious behavior.

Does it make sense now why you see many homeless people in the major cities of The United States of America? They have a violent expression of evil upon themselves. Until they come from out under the curse, they will never have the gift of God's grace upon their lives. It is not because they are worthless people, it is because they have a violent expression of evil upon their lives. Not just evil, but a violent expression of evil. Whatever they touch with their hands turns to a violent expression of evil. Since God cannot stand evil, He in reality, is not near that person. He or she are fighting life's battles alone.

Many times, curse upon our lives is the fruit of choices made by others around us. God promises to be near to the brokenhearted, and will provide a way for you to get out from under the curse— homeless or rich young rulers alike.

On the other hand, the person who is operating under blessing touches something with their hands and it prospers to the glory of God. Since God can stand goodness, He is near that person as they fight life's battles. He would never leave you or forsake you. A guard upon your life twenty-four seven!

When you understand that God cursed this world and the only way to stay out from under the curse is through your obedience to God: you will do all you can to be obedient to God and please Him. Only a fool would enjoy being a violent expression of evil. Because they are ignorant to the things of God, there are many foolish people in the world who are operating with a violent expression of evil upon there lives.

Are you foolish? If you have asked Jesus to be your Lord, please do not be named among the foolish people of the world. If you are foolish then you are operating in life with a violent expression of evil upon your life. The curse is to be forbidden upon God's people (Gen. 12:3).

But God will not go against your will, if you choose to operate with a violent expression of evil upon your life, and God will not force you to accept His gift of grace. The choice is yours! Do you want success in your life? God tells you how to obtain success in life. Meditate upon His book (The Bible) day and night and do not let words move away from your eyes. Ponder His ways and study His directions and life will always be a blessing to you.

Chapter Fourteen

Reality of the Lord

We need to take a look at the word Lord. What does the word mean? In the Strong's, it's defined as a title of majesty and kingship. As applied to Christ, kyrios indicates Christ's Lordship ("Jesus as Lord"). Jesus is to have absolute Lordship over our lives. Then what does Lordship mean? Again in the Strong's it's supreme authority.

Why then are people today who have been born again into the Body of Christ not giving Jesus supreme authority over their lives? Because they do not recognize Jesus as supreme authority. What did Satan tell Eve? If she'd eat the fruit, she could be like God—or have supreme authority over her own life. Someone has to have supreme authority over your life, either God or Satan. Satan starts off with the authority when you are born into the earth, but if you come into the reality of the Lord, you change authority from Satan to the Lord.

Most people have confessed Jesus as Savior, but have not made Him Lord. We must allow Jesus to be the supreme authority in our lives. There are many reasons behind someone not knowing that Jesus is to have supreme authority in their life, but because God is God, there is only one person who will answer to the Lord—you.

Earlier I said to study to show yourself approved unto God. If you do not recognize someone as having supreme authority over you, then you cannot give that person supreme authority over you. The Bible says all liars will be thrown into the lake of fire. You might say that you are not a liar, but the Bible defines liars as manifestation of untruth.

Some examples are denial that Jesus is Christ, not keeping Christ's commandments, hating one's brother, those who speak wickedness, false witnesses, and astrologers. You might ask yourself the following question: What does all this have to do with the reality of the Lord? If Jesus is your

Lord you will not speak wickedness, hate one's brother, deny Jesus is Christ, and will keep Christ's commandments.

You put all your trust in Christ Jesus and not in yourself. You allow Him to rule your life in every way possible. You come to the Lord in childlike faith. Jesus' way is the only way for your life. You find Christians in litigation all the time, but Christ warns against it (Matt. 5:25, 40). You see Christians in litigation against other Christians. Christ gives a warning, and Paul who was under the anointing of the Holy Spirit of God also gives a warning against filing lawsuits (1 Cor 6:1, 2).

Then what commandment of Christ's am I not keeping? To love one another as Christ loved us. If you are filing a lawsuit against another brother or sister in Christ, does that show the love of God? Why do brothers and sisters file lawsuit? Because they do not know what the Word of God says about the subject, or they do not believe what the Word of God says about the subject, or they do not care what the Word of God says about the subject.

If you knew the reality of the Lord, you would stop that lawsuit against another brother or sister in the Body of Christ. They may have hurt you, and legal action seems justified, but the Word tells us that we are not to go before a judge to bring an lawsuit against another brother or sister. If it is too late, if you have already done it, you can ask for repentance of the Lord. What is more important to you? Suing someone in court, or obeying the commandments of the Lord? If you choose suing someone in court, go ahead with your rebellious self.

If you choose to obey the commandments of the Lord, you made the right choice. Go to the head of the class! You now know the reality of the Lord. What is the reality of the Lord? Obeying the Lord is the reality of the Lord. If you respect someone, you will obey them. You confirm the reality of that person in your life by obeying them.

Kids who don't obey their parents are not confirming the reality of their parents in their life, nor are they confirming the reality of the Lord in their life. Because the Lord gives each child a commandment to obey their parents. Respect and obedience go hand in hand. If you respect someone, you will obey them, and if you obey someone you respect them. If you respect and obey the Lord, you bring the reality of the Lord into your life. He becomes real to you! When you respect someone you won't just do anything around that person. When you respect the Lord, you will not just do anything, your life will mirror the Lord's. He is our example and your life will follow the example He established.

The Lord did not fornicate; so, why do we fornicate? The Lord did not steal; why then do we steal? Fornicating and stealing are action words, but when we take action not to do either, we bring the reality of the Lord into our lives. The Lord forgave easily. When we do not forgive; we are not operating in the reality of the Lord. He forgave, so we much also forgive.

What is the reality of the Lord? That it is no longer you who is living, but it is Christ who is alive in you. The Lord did not worry. When you worry you are in sin and sin is not of the Lord. Sin hinders the reality of the Lord manifesting in your life. Many a great man and woman of God never got to the promised land, because of hidden sin in their life that stopped the reality of the Lord from being manifested in their lives.

Stop! I do not want you to go any further without examining yourself for the Body and for the Blood. When you take time out to examine yourself; you can't help but to find yourself right in the middle of the reality of the Lord for your life.

Stop! It is time to truly examine yourself. What goal did you not make? If you will not examine yourself, then what place does Christ have in you? The answer to that question is none. If you will not take the time to examine yourself to see if the reality of the Lord is alive in you then you are a scared, unforgiving, unkind, and insecure person. Take the time to examine yourself to see if the reality of the Lord is alive in you. He will strengthen you to face whatever it is that you are afraid of.

The reality of the Lord will cause you to stop stealing from your boss at work. It will cause you to make up lost time when you come in late. It will cause you to be friendly to the person who hates you. It will cause you to be a Christian!

When you understand the reality of the Lord in your life, it will cause you to see yourself as God sees you. How does God see you? God sees you as an overcomer in life. God sees you as the head and not the tail. God sees you as above and not beneath. God sees you as a world overcomer. God sees you as blessed and empowered to prosper in life. The reality of the Lord keeps you asking, seeking, and knocking.

Luke 11:9, says, So I say to you, ask, and it will be given to you; seek, and you will find; knock, and it will be opened to you.

I do not know about you; but I do not have time to play games with the Lord. I must ask, seek, and knock until, I find the reality of the Lord in my life. I will do everything that is required in order to have the Reality of the Lord operating in my life. It is no longer I who live, but Christ is alive in me and I now know the reality of the Lord.

The three imperatives (ask, seek, and knock) are in the Greek present tense, denoting a continuous asking, seeking, and knocking. In order for the true Reality of the Lord to happen in my life, I must continue asking, seeking, and knocking until the Lord reveals to me all that He wants to tell me. I can't ask one day and not ask the next day. We must ask each and every day until the revelation of the Lord is revealed. The reality of the Lord or the revelation of the Lord will be revealed to the person who is thirsty for the Lord.

Do not get me wrong everyone will experience some level of the reality of the Lord; but the person who is thirsty for the presence of the Lord will reach the last level of the reality of the Lord. That person will know the Lord in a personal way. This is the level that I want to get to. I want all of God.

Have you experienced the Lord in a way that you can say, "He is seating here with me at this very moment?" God wants us to be so full of Him, that people will say that we are drunk. If you are drunk in the Holy Spirit, there is nothing else that can come upon you.

When you are full of God; you will know the reality of the Lord. When you know the reality of the Lord that business deal that seemed to never get off the ground before suddenly gets off the ground and you go from just making it in sales, to overflowing in sales. When you are full of the presence of God; the boss who'd never looked your way is now paying you plenty of attention, and favor is overtaking you where ever you go.

When you know the reality of the Lord; your steps are ordered of the Lord and He takes you and puts you on His back and carries you to the finish line. When you know the reality of the Lord, everything that you touch with your hand prospers. When you know the reality of the Lord, your mistakes are blessed. When you know the reality of the Lord, everyone in your new company gets a pink slip except you. They find you a new job! What am I saying? Just this; when you know the reality of the Lord nothing can go wrong for You.

You might say that is impossible. You are right! But don't you know that nothing is impossible for God? When you know the reality of the Lord nothing is impossible for God. We serve a big God not some small, unconcerned God. Not only is our God big, but He is concerned about our smallest need.

The God of the universe has taken the time to reveal Himself to us. When we take the time to know the reality of the Lord, He will reveal Himself to us. Folks, we are not talking about some dead God, I am talking about the living God, who made the Heavens and earth; the great and awesome God; the God of Isaac, Abraham and Jacob wants to know you and me in a personal way.

I count it an honor to know the Reality of the Lord. We have not chosen ourselves, He has chosen us. We know the Yankees, we know the Mets, we know the Lakers, and we know the Kings, but do we know the King of kings?

Do you know the King of kings in a personal manner? If you do know the King of kings in a personal manner, then you know the reality of the Lord. I am not talking about knowing His Name. The reality of the Lord takes on a different meaning when you know who He is: Do you know Him as Jehovah

Rohi our Shepherd? Do you know Him as Jehovah Tsidkenu our Righteousness. Do you know Him as Elohim our Creator? Do you know Him as El Shaddai God Almighty? Do you know Him at Adonai my Lord? Do you know Him as Jehovah Jireh our provider? Do you know Him as Jehovah Rophe our healer? Do you know Him as Jehovah Nissi our banner? Do you know Him as Jehovah M'Kaddesh our sanctifier? Do you know Him as Jehovah Shalom our peace?

If you know Him as any of these, then and only then can you say that you know the reality of the Lord. See He is our Creator, Banner, Shepherd, Righteousness, Provider, Healer, and Sanctifier. If you do not know Him as any of the names; then how do you get to know Him? The answer is fellowship. You must fellowship with the Lord in order to know Him. If you need peace in your life right now.

Can you go to Jehovah Shalom and ask for Him to provide you with His peace? The peace you desire is in Jehovah Shalom's presence. In the presence of the Lord is everything we want or need. If you do not know the reality of the Lord, you will not know that everything you ever desired is already in place in the presence of the Lord. In Jesus is peace, healing, and provision!

Jesus provided for all mankind's every need on the cross. It is up to mankind to come to the place were we ask for what already belongs to us. The store was paid for by the priceless blood of Jesus. We have been bought back from the devil. He no longer can claim you as his. You are the property of the Father God through the priceless blood of Jesus.

When you know who you are In Christ; then you will know the reality of the Lord. You must first know who you are in Christ. God's says His people perish for a lack of knowledge. You must know who you are in Christ. In Christ, there is freedom from the sin, of law and death. In Christ, you are no longer under the curse of the law. I beg you to seek and study the Word of God so you can know it for yourself. The Reality of the Lord is your key to the promises of God. The Lord will not withhold anything from you in His presence.

Get into the presence of God so you can experience all that God as for you. There is joy in the presence of God! There is wisdom, direction, and understanding in the presence of God. In the presence of God, the Reality of the Lord is revealed. I am going to repeat it: In the presence of God is revealed the Reality of the Lord.

Where do you want to be? If you desire the presence of God, then get ready to experience the reality of the Lord. Your steps will be order in the presence of God, that will cause you to walk in the reality of the Lord like you never, never, never, walked before. The journey is sweet and the trip is long. Hang on, the Holy Spirit will be your guide. Do not try to guide yourself.

He has more experience than you and is able to show you the holes in the runway as you take off.

He is the copilot, but will not take control until you let go of control. If you agree to let the Holy Spirit have control of the joystick then we can get started. I know you will fly in life with the Holy Spirit in charge. He will take you right to the plains of the reality of the Lord. He will make your landing smooth, so that life's battles will never overtake you. He never said you would not have battles. He will make sure that they do not overtake you. The journey will take a lifetime to complete, but in the end, if you let Him control things, you will hear the Lord of Reality say to you Well done my good and faithful servant enter into the joy of the Lord.

Chapter Fifteen

Believe the Report of The Lord

What are you believing God for? If you are not believing God for anything, that is one of the worst position to be in. God owns the universe! He is the One who has it all.

I want to challenge your belief patterns. What are you believing? Are you believing that the God of the universe who made the Heavens and earth is your provider? Are you believing that the God of the universe, who made the Heavens and earth can do anything? Are you believing that He who raised Jesus from the dead can heal you from the disease of cancer?

What are you believing? If you are not believing what the Word of God says, then you probably are believing a lie. The devil will lie to Christians as well as non-Christians. It does not matter who you are. If he lied to Eve when she was in the Garden of Eden, he will lie to you today.

Why do they call cancer a disease? Looking at the word disease you can see, if you will look closely. Disease, if the dis is taken off becomes ease. God wants each of us to be at ease. What is another word for ease? Another word for ease is peace. If you are told you have cancer of the breast, you will probably not be at peace. If you know the Word of God, you can be at ease when you receive such alarming information. Why? Because Jesus bore all of our sicknesses and disease on the cross 2000 years ago. Healing is part of the salvation package you received, if and when you received Jesus into your heart. 1 Peter 2:24, says; Who Himself bore our sins in His own body on the tree, that we, having died to sins, might live for righteousness —by whose stripes you were healed.

Another reason we are to believe the report of the Lord and not the report of the world is found also in 1 Peter. We are not to worry because the Father's love provides for both our daily needs and our special needs. Would you not agree that being told you have cancer is a special need that needs to be addressed?

1 Peter 5:7, says; Casting all your care upon Him, for He cares for you. The word care in the Greek is merimna. The word denotes distractions, anxieties, burdens, and worries. He doesn't say that worries, burdens, and distractions will not come; what He is saying is that when they come, cast them upon Jesus. That is so important!

Again, I ask you what are you believing?

If you believe the Word of God, you will in a heartbeat cast all the cares of this world upon the Lord. If there is any doubt in you, one of two things will happen: (1) You will not cast any cares upon he Lord; or (2) You will cast some of the cares, but not all of your cares.

In which one of these places do you find yourself? I hope that I do not find you in any of those places. I hope you believe the Word of God. Life's burdens are designed to keep you away from God's promises.

Jesus will not come to earth again to prove it to you. He puts men and women in our paths to help us get to where He wants us to go. But often, we reject the men and women that are put in our paths. Do you believe that God wants you to be set apart from the world? Holiness is just that; being holy is being set apart unto God and from the world. Do you live so unbelievers will give God glory, because your life is righteous?

Does your life cause your unbelieving coworkers to wonder if you are a Christian or not? What are you believing?

If your walk is not right because of what you are believing, the Word of God has the answer for you. 1 John 2:6, says; He who says he abides in Him ought himself also to walk just as He walked.

How did He walk? In obedience to His Father. We should walk the same way. If we did, there would never be a question of what we believe.

You receive a report that you have been fired from your job that you have held for over 20 years. What should be your response? Whose report are you going to believe? If you walk the same walk that Jesus walked, then your response and report will be that God's has a better job for you and a promotion to go along with the job. You will stand on 1 Peter 5:7 until the job manifests itself. Many times, we want to give up, but brothers and sisters, stand and stand until you see the glory of God. Do not give up!

If is just a two letter word, but a very powerful word. The word denotes your choice in life. If you choose to not believe the Word of God, you put yourself under the curse. If you choose to believe the Word of God, you put yourself under the blessing. God does not limit your freedom of choice. He allows you to choose to be blessed or cursed. You choose what path in life you are going down.

What are you believing? Both Christians and non-Christians blame God for accidents, deaths, and all other tragic things in life. That is without thinking! If you would stop and think for just one moment: Who came to kill, and steal in life? Was it God or was it the devil? Most people know the answer—the devil.

Then why are you blaming God for accidents, deaths, and all the other tragic things that happen in life? This world does not want to cast the blame on the real character, who for years has gone untouched by the world—the devil. He is the one who causes accidents, early deaths, and all other tragic things in life. The blame belongs in his lap not God's.

Again, who are you going to believe? If, you are going to believe God; know that all the blessings of Abraham are yours for the taking. If you choose to believe the devil; know that all the curses of the devil are yours for the taking. Life is associated with God and death is associated with the devil. You make the choice! While you are thinking about who you will choose, I want you to read this Scripture:

And whatever we ask we receive from Him, because we keep His commandments and do those things that are pleasing in His sight (John 3:22).

Notice it did not say our sight. We are to do those things which are pleasing in His sight. If you purpose in your heart to do those things which are pleasing in His sight, you cannot go wrong. Whatever we ask for, we receive from Him.

If your son or daughter is pleasing in your sight, whatever they ask from you, they receive from you. You do not mind giving them whatever they ask, if they are pleasing in your sight. That is just how our Heavenly Father feels. If we are pleasing in His sight, we shall receive from Him whatever we ask.

You might be saying, I have not received from Him what I have been asking for. There is a qualifier! Does what you been asking for line up with the will of God? You cannot ask for some other person's wife. That is called adultery, and it does not line up with the will of God. You cannot ask for the person that hurt you to go far from your presence. That is called unforgiveness, and it does not line up with the will of God. God requires you to forgive those who have hurt you. If you are married, He has given you your own wife. If you choose to believe the promise outlined in 1 John 3:22, and you line your actions and words up with the will of God, you will be on top of the world.

You will be the head and not the tail! When we keep His commandments we give evidence that we are in harmony with God's will. Again, what are you believing? It is so important that what you allow yourself to believe lines up with the will of God. God has given us His will in His Word. The Bible contains all of the will of God. It is there for you to examine to the fullest.

Many people do not own a Bible in their home. When I was growing up everyone owned a Bible in their home. It may have collected dust, but it was in almost every home. The United States of America has drifted so far from God that a full fledged turn back to God is the only thing that will save this country.

Is what you have been believing sin? You might say, I just have not been believing the Word of God—that is not sin. Well, lets describe the word sin. Sin is disobedience of God's law. If you are not believing God's Word, you are disobedient to God's law, because God's law is God's Word! You can't get around that fact of truth—God's law is God's Word. Cut it any way you want to and it will come up the same way—God's law is God's Word.

If you have not been fully believing God's Word you have been sinning. 1 John 3:9, says; Whoever has been born of God does not sin, for His seed remains in him; and he cannot sin, because he has been born of God.

Sin is natural to children of the devil, who have sinned from the beginning, but unnatural to children of God, who cannot sin without the Spirit's conviction. A constant indulgence in sin contradicts the claim to have a personal knowledge of Christ. Christians are able to commit an occasional act of sin, but they are not characterized by the spirit of lawlessness. When they do sin, God has given us 1 John 1:9 to get back in right fellowship with Him.

Now that we know that sin is disobedience to the law of God and that God's law is God's Word— we need to believe the Word of God with all our heart. There are spiritual laws that are lay down in the Word of God for all to follow. It does not matter if you believe what is written. The only thing that matters is that they are there for all to read and follow.

Do you know that you will be accountable for the Word of God even if you haven't read the Bible? You will be held accountable for something that you may or may not know. God has given us His Word to follow. The most important book that you can every read and understand is the Bible. The Word of God tells us that we have a better covenant and better promises. Again, I ask what are you believing? In Hebrews 8:6, it says:

But now, He has obtained a more excellent ministry, inasmuch as He is also Mediator of a better covenant, which was established on better promises.

Who is He? Jesus! Jesus has obtained a better covenant, which was established on better promises and He is the Mediator. Jesus' present day ministry is more excellent than the ministry He had while He walked upon the earth.

Do you see that also? The Scripture says He obtained a more excellent ministry. Jesus had a ministry when He walked the earth, but His present day ministry is more excellent then the one before, not just excellent, but more excellent.

God does not just make up words, He wants you to not only see something, but learn something in His Word. All the more reason why we should believe the Word of God to the fullest. The devil tried to kill Jesus and all that happened was Jesus did not remain dead, but was raised up to another level. He had a ministry when He walked the earth, and now seated in Heaven, He has a more excellent ministry.

The Scriptures says; He obtained a more excellent ministry. If cancer comes your way do you believe the cancer report or do you tap into the more excellent ministry of Jesus? Whose report will you believe? The report of the earthly doctor or the report of the Great doctor—King Jesus? The report of the earthly doctor may contain facts, but the report of the Great doctor will contain truths.

Whatever you are believing will dictate your path in life. If you believe the tradition of man or the lies of the devil you place yourself in the position to obtain death as your reward. If you do not believe the tradition of man or the lies of the devil, but the Word of God, you place yourself in the position to obtain life as your reward. Which one these rewards will you obtain?

What you believe or do not believe is firmly in your hands. You can make your life a success, or you can make your life a failure. You are the one in charge, not the devil or God. Make the most of this once in a lifetime deal.

Jesus is our Mediator. Mediation is a friendly intervention designed to render assistance. We can't go wrong if we line up with the Word of God and follow it. If you are following Him and abiding in the Word, Jesus is intervening for you. With the friendly intervention of Jesus, you can't go wrong. Now, Jesus is also our High Priest. Let's see, what the Word of God says about Jesus being our High Priest: Now this is the main point of the things we are saying: We have such a High Priest, who is seated at the right hand of the throne of the Majesty in the Heavens; a Minister of the sanctuary and of the true tabernacle which the Lord erected, and not man (Heb. 8:12), God does not use empty words, He is making a statement in the Word above. God makes it plain that the main point He wants to get across to us is that in the more excellent ministry of Jesus, we have a High Priest who is seated with authority. See for yourself, Now this is the main point of the things we are saying: We have such a High Priest....

Again, what are you believing? Are you believing you have cancer, when we have a High Priest who is seated at the right hand of the throne of majesty in the Heavens and has a Name that is above every name? I want to ask you a question. Is cancer a name? If you have not claimed His Name for yourself, then He is not your High Priest.

Back to the more excellent ministry and the blood-cleansed. We can't go wrong if we will follow closely the protection (security) of the Lord. I want you to understand this one point: The payment for our security was the blood of Jesus. He paid an awesome price for your security.

The story of the three Hebrew young men is a dramatic illustration of the personal presence and protection of the Lord for His people who suffer for their testimony. The fourth man in the furnace is a Christophany (preincarnate appearance of the Messiah) whom even the king recognized to be like the Son of God. Nebuchadnezzar acknowledged that the deliverance was of God.

Your enemies will acknowledge that your deliverance is of God when you live, move, and have your being in fellowship with the Father, the Son, and the Holy Spirit. One last thing that fasting, praying, and praising should be in your life as they will bring obedience into your life. You cannot do all three on a regular basis and not be obedient.

The Spirit of Obedience will chase you down! If you are fasting, praying, and praising you are on the road to having the security of the Godly upon your life on a daily basis. Do not get caught up in denominations, but get caught up in relationship with God the Father, God's ministry.

What does more mean—something in addition. What does excellent mean—the very best of its kind. What was added to the very good ministry of Jesus? I believe what was added to Jesus' ministry is you and me.

Let me tell you how I came this theory: When our Lord walked the earth, His ministry was very good. One reference that backs this up is the statement that Jesus went about doing good and healing all that were sick. Jesus is the head over the Church—you and me. We were added to the good ministry of Jesus; who is the go between for mankind and God.

Jesus did not have a Church while, He walked on this earth. The Church—called out ones; was not added until Jesus went back to be with the Father.

If you can, get this in your spirit—our High Priest is waiting for us to call upon Him, and He will, through the Holy Spirit, by the Father, help us. Jesus' ministry is performed in the true sanctuary, not of Earth, but of Heaven. As Priest and King, He occupies the place of Supreme power. Are you fearing that your unsaved love ones cannot be saved? If so, you do not know the power of Jesus' present day more excellent ministry. The power of Jesus' present day more excellent ministry is awesome, just awesome.

We do not have to believe anything outside of the Word of God. The Bible spells out all the things that Jesus' present day more excellent ministry can, and will do for you. If you choose to believe things outside of the Word of God; you are taking a serious risk. A risk that can lead to death! I am not trying to frighten you; I am trying to inform you.

Jesus Christ came into history as an eternal Priest to offer an eternal sacrifice for sin. The shedding of His blood provided a permanent sacrifice and a permanent covenant bond between God and man. His blood was applied not merely to an earthly altar, but to the very altar of God in Heaven, where, once and for all, it obtained redemption for sin for those who receive Him. The immutable bond that is established through the New Covenant in Christ's blood is the ultimate fulfillment of God's covenant-making nature. Grace and mercy characterized the new covenant replacing the inadequate first covenant.

Why am I telling you this? Because you have rights in the new covenant. Rights that affect what you believe and what you do not believe. It is your right for all of your household to be saved (new covenant). It is your right for you to walk in the divine health of the Lord (new covenant). It is your right to prosper (new covenant). It is your right to be healed (new covenant). It is your right to speak with other tongues (new covenant). It is your right to grow (new covenant). It is your right to be unafraid (new covenant). It is your right to be humble and uplifted (new covenant). It is your right, swift to hear (new covenant).

You might be saying, I have a problem with healing and with other tongues. Are you going to believe the tradition of people or the Word of God? Which one is the authority in your life?

Remember this, If you do not believe the Word of God you are sinning. If you only believe part of the Word of God you are sinning. You are responsible for what you believe or do not believe. You must search the Bible to find out what the will of God is. Anything short of this produces sin in your life.

You cannot place one foot on the property of the devil and one foot on the property of God and expect a miracle to happen in your life. You must believe the Word of God in order for miracles to happen in your life! You must believe the Word of God in order for you to receive the blessings of God into your life.

Sin is disobedience of God's Law. What is sin defined as, biblically? Transgression (1 John 3:4), Unrighteousness (1 John 5:17), Omission of known duty (Jas. 4:17), Not from Faith (Rom. 5:12, 16), Thought of foolishness (Prov. 24:9).

What are some types of sin? National (Prov. 14:34), Personal (Josh. 7:20), Secret (Ps. 90:8), Willful (Ps. 19:13), Obvious (1 Tim. 5:24); Shameless (Is. 3:9); Youthful/immature (Ps. 25:7); Public (2 Sam. 24:10, 17); Unforgivable (Matt. 12:21, 32, John 8:24); Of ignorance (Lev. 4:2); Determination (Heb. 10:26).

Do I mean to tell you that you can be sinning through your ignorance? Failure to observe the commandments of the Lord results in a violation in the holiness code and in the covenant relationship with God. It does not say you must know the commandment, even those God holds you responsible for knowing what the commandment is saying.

You are held accountable for what you unintentionally do not know concerning the commandments of the Lord. Why, because, He tells you to seek His Kingdom and His righteousness.

Chapter Sixteen

The Security of the Godly

We have security if we are the godly. Angels will be encamped around us to keep us in all our ways. We will abide under the wings of the Almighty. What a special place to abide. What greater protection is there for the godly than under the wings of the Almighty?

Psalm 91:1, says, He who dwells in the secret place of the Most High shall remain stable and fixed under the shadow of the Almighty. In this verse there are two names of God: the Most High or El Elyon and the Almighty or El Shaddai.

Recently. I lost my cell phone on the way to work but within 30 minutes, El Elyon was on the job, advising my wife were my cell phone was. My wife called my cell phone number to see if I was at work yet. She had just let me off at work at 7:30 a.m. and the Sheriff's Department answered my cell phone at 8:00 a.m. My wife not knowing that I had lost my cell phone hung up.

I want you to see what Psalm 91:11-12 had to say: "For He shall give His angels charge over you. To keep you in all your ways. In their hands they shall bear you up, Lest you dash your foot against a stone.

He shall give His angels charge over you. I did not know for sure that I had lost my cell phone, but immediately God had my wife call the number and we were able to know actually where my cell phone was. Whoever found the phone turned it into the Deputy Sheriff.

The Most High God is concerned about every area of your life. This might not seem much to you, but I know of another employee at my job who's husband lost his cell phone at work. Someone got it and charged over $200 worth of calls, plus they had to pay for another activation fee.

God's protection is great. We did not have to pay for anything. The phone was lost on Friday, and I had it back in my possession on Monday. I am not saying that I am better than the other gentleman, but that if you will abide in His Word, He will take care of your every need and want.

My cell phone could have been replaced, but God the Father does not want you to be concerned with anything. I am not saying either, that the other gentleman is not seeking the Kingdom of God, what I am saying that I know, that I know that my wife and I are seeking the Kingdom of God and His righteousness with all our hearts, our soul, and our minds. Since we are seeking the Kingdom of God and His righteousness with every fiber of our being, then God is obligated to take care of us. I am not boasting. The Word of God says that, our needs will be met if we seek first the Kingdom of God and His righteousness. The security of the Godly can take on many forms. One such form is that you can seem to finish your job tasks quicker then others. God can help you not used as much energy as others in accomplishing your task. We overlook the security of God toward His people. Looking back how He protected Israel. He will protect us today.

I can recall coming home from church and a little girl ran in front of my van. I did not have time to stop, but that young child was placed back on the sidewalk and kept on going. God protected not only that young child, but me and my family as well. Proverbs 18:10; says, The name of the Lord is a strong tower. The righteous run to it and are safe. The original says, The name of the Lord is a strong tower. The righteous run to it and are set on high.

If you are set on high, nothing, and I mean nothing can get to you. You are secure when you run to the name of the Lord. There is power and protection in the name of the Lord. Jesus paid a awesome price for the name Lord Jesus. You do not realize the price that Jesus paid for the right to be called Lord by you and I. He gave His life. Jesus' life was not taken from Him. He laid it down so that we could have abundant life. If I had hit that young child, her parents would be without a daughter and I would be suffering from the pain of having caused the death of that child.

We called on the Name of Jesus in that van, and He sent His angels to protect that van and the young child. She never realized that she was put back on the sidewalk, but we knew what had just taken place. If we had not spoken out the name of Jesus, I believe we would have hit that young child.

The name of the Lord is your strong tower; not just a tower, but a strong tower. God wants us to know the security of the godly is in that strong tower. He wants us to know that once we are in, no one can pluck us out.

Not everyone can run into the name of the Lord. The name of the Lord is reserved for the righteous, and only the righteous. Who are the righteous? They are the ones who are upright before God. God does not protect openly those whom are not upright before Him. He promises protection to the righteous. The righteous may run into His Name and be kept safe. The name of the Lord protects not only by strength, but also by height. The righteous are lifted out of reach. You have nothing to fear when your protection comes from the Lord.

The righteous are children of the Most High God (El Elyon) who have declared themselves upright because of their thoughts and deeds. When you give your all to the Lord, the Lord will give His all to you. You can't beat God's generosity, no matter how hard you try. Keep on giving to God and God will keep on giving to you. Proverbs 16:3 could not make it any more plain, Commit your works to the Lord. And your thoughts will be established.

If one turns over to the Lord what he plans to do, his life purposes will come to fruition. You can't beat this kind of security. Your purpose for living will be protected when you turn your plans over to the Lord. If that isn't security, I do not know what it is. God will take your thoughts and make them come to pass.

I know we do not think of that as security of the godly, but it is just that. The Lord has given you a promise! If you will take your works and thoughts and roll them to the Lord, He will—not shall— but will make them come to fruition or pass. The stock market could crash, but your stocks will not. Why? Because, you committed your works to the Lord and He's established them. We must get to the point were we believe the Word of God. You might ask, how can my stocks rise when the stock market just went belly up? Because, you have committed your stocks to the Lord and He established the plan that your stocks would take in life.

If you don't believe this, just read your Bible. God will always prosper His people in the time of famine. You have security when you know that you know that, God is protective of His people; that everything that you touch with your hands will prosper to the glory of God.

It shall come to pass when you roll all your plans over to the Lord. The security of the godly cannot be shown to you with any greater force than what is found in Proverbs 16:3.

Believe the Word of God and your very life purposes will come to fruition. You can believe the facts of the world, or you can believe the truth of the Word of God. It is a fact of this world that cancer is present, but the truth of the Word of God is that by the very stripes of Jesus you are healed. Which of these will you allow to dominate your life? What are you allowing to dominate your life? The facts of this world want first place.

I am not saying that you do not go to the doctor. God made doctors for us! What I am saying is that the truth of God's Word says that by the stripes of Jesus you have been made whole. It is up to you to by faith get this in your being. You were healed 2000 years ago on Calvary! When Jesus' redemptive work was finished, it was finished for all of mankind.

All is all. It includes all that were living at that time and all that would come in the future. What part of all do you not understand?

On the cross Jesus said, "It is finished." You might say, But I feel like I am sick, Faith is not a feeling; it is by faith that you must claim your healing, before it can manifest it self in your life.

When Jesus said, "It is finished," He proclaimed all the redemptive work was complete. Faith comes by hearing the Word of God. The Word of God is alive and will prosper in your life if allowed.

Healing is security! If you are sick you feel insecure. If you are well you feel secure. When you are healed, you experience the security of the godly. You might be saying, I am well, but are you saved?

There are only two kinds of people in this world: the saved and the unsaved. You have either accepted the redemptive work of Jesus and asked Him to be the Lord and Savior of your life, or you have not accepted the redemptive work of Jesus and have not asked Him to be the Lord and Savior of your life. If you are saved, then you have the security of the Godly upon your life, if you are unsaved, then you do not have the security of the Godly upon your life.

That is the bad news, but the good news is you do not have to stay the unsaved. The free gift of salvation is waiting for you! One part of this gift is healing. Healing was purchased for you by Jesus' stripes. Why do you trample over the blood of Jesus by not accepting healing as part of the package of salvation?

By Jesus' stripes you were healed. If you are healed then you are healed. Not yesterday or the next day, but right this moment, you are healed. Just reach out and claim your healing by faith.

Faith is an action word—you must do something. You have so much in God that you do not know what you have. God the Father is just that, a Father. He loves us so much that all the steps have been taken for us to enjoy completed freedom from the enemy of our soul. All we must do is believe. If we would believe God's Word then we would be so secure in God, that No weapons formed against us will prosper (Isa. 54:17).

It is a truth that there is one Body of Christ, but the fact is that there are many denominations. What should be the governing law for any denomination? The Word of God! Not what someone in the past thought was the Word. I am against denominational segregation.

Before you put this book down let me explain myself. Let's look at this word: denomination. Denomination is the direct difference of nomination. When you nominate someone or something then you are for it. In reality, the word denomination means you are against someone or something. We have used the denomination wrongly over these years.

The people that came up with the idea of forming denominations/ nations, were in reality against the Body of Christ. Study the Word! You will not find any Baptists or any other denomination mentioned in Scripture. John the Baptist is the only reference to Baptists in Scripture. In the beginning, we were not called Christians either.

I will let you in on a secret: If you are in a group and know nothing about its bylaws you are lost. You must know the Bible.

The Church of the Lord Jesus is made up of all nations! Paul warned us that evil men would come into the Church to cause division among the Body. When the Church was together on Pentecost, they experienced power. Why? Because they were of one accord. The Body of Christ must get back to being of one accord. Therein lies the security of godly.

I believe the reason we don't see the security of the godly at all times is because of the division in the Body of Christ. We are called to be brothers and sisters, not denominations. We can disagree, but we have one thing in common: the blood of Jesus has purchased us all. The blood of Jesus paid for our security of the Godly. The only reason we have this security is the blood of Jesus. Nothing but the blood of Jesus cleanse us whiter then snow.

God did not call us out of the kingdom of darkness and place us in the Kingdom of His dear Son for us to be placed in denominations. Think a minute about a secure vault. You are placed in a vault, not several different vaults. God saved us to place us in the Body of Christ, not several denominations. Denominations are man made! In the security of the godly is fellowship.

The devil fed us a lie years ago, and we took it hook, line, and sinker. Get this! What denomination do you belong to? In other words what part of God's Word are you against? We have allowed the devil to have too much room in the Body of Christ. He does not belong in the real Church of Jesus Christ. God's ways are higher then our ways and His thoughts are higher then our thoughts. God never gave us permission to start denominations, He said go into all the nations and baptize them in the name of the Father, the Son, and the Holy Ghost, and told us to make of all men disciples. A disciple means a student! What are they learning? To be secure in the Kingdom of God.

Denominations are religious organizations uniting local congregations in a single body. God never called us into a religious organization; He called us into fellowship with His Son, Jesus Christ. We are not to be in an organization, but in a relationship. Those three Hebrews young men come to mind once again, Shadrach, Meshach, and AbedNego. Daniel 3:28 reads: Nebuchadnezzar spoke, saying, "Blessed be the God of Shadrach, Meshach, and AbedNego, who sent His Angel and delivered His servants who trusted in Him, and they have frustrated the king's word, and yielded their bodies, that they should not serve nor worship any god except their own God!"

When you are in relationship with the God of the universe, you are in good hands. No one can keep you like God! If you don't know the story the three were put into the king's furnace for not worshipping the king's god. If any time in history were the security of the Godly is shown, then it is now.

Not only are they secure from the fierce furnace, but they find favor with King Nebuchadnezzar. Nebuchadnezzar's favor is bestowed upon the three. Nebuchadnezzar acknowledged that their deliverance was of God. If you will only stand firm and see the glory of God, all your friends, enemies, and coworkers will acknowledge the security of the Godly.

God will never let us down. If He kept Shadrach, Meshach, and AbedNego, He will keep you in the midst of the fire in your life. You do not have to go into battle alone. The battle is not yours, the battle is the Lord's. Can you see that? Your job is to continue to stand in faith and God's job is to bless.

If you will not be shaken in your faith, you will see the glory of God manifested in your life. In 2 Chronicles, Chapter 20 is probably the most familiar and loved chapter, for it explains how the Lord grants victory to those who trust in Him.

Jehoshaphat was facing the greatest external threat of his reign. A great multitude of Moabites, Ammonites, and others from Syria were plotting to crush Judah. In the face of these incredible odds, Jehoshaphat humbled himself before the Lord; and the result was the greatest victory he had ever experienced.

The promise of the Lord, through the prophet Jahaziel, is a comfort to believers of all ages who face hopeless situations. Do not be afraid or dismayed…for the battle is not yours, but God's (2 Chron.20:15). However, the account reveals three key elements that put God's people in the place where He could deliver them: 1) fasting; 2) prayer; and 3) praise.

These three elements will bring the security in place in moment's notice. Fasting is simply an outward indication of an inward sincerity, evidence of the urgency we feel when many brothers and sisters have been taken captive into the financial POW camp.

Because of tradition, we have been taught that it is holy to be poor and that God does not want you to have wealth. But you shall (earnestly) remember the Lord your God, for it is He Who gives you power to get wealth, that He may establish His covenant which He swore to your fathers, as it is this day (Deut. 8:18).

God wants you to have wealth in order to aid in His covenant being established in your life. How can the glory of God be shown in you if you are broke?

You see Churches that have bake sales or yard sales, but God never called for His Body to have sales. In Deuteronomy 8:18, God tells us that He gives the church power to get wealth that He may establish His covenant.

I hear your unbelief. The people sought God in prayer and with faith in His Word. The victory came in a strange, but powerful manner. The Levites stood and praised the Lord God of Israel with voices loud and high. The result of this powerful praise was total victory. The security of God will follow those who learn to fast, pray, and praise the Lord God of Israel.

God is enthroned in the praises of His people. Whenever and wherever God's people praise Him, He reigns among them and does miraculous things on their behalf, If so much was done for the people of the Old Testament, then how much more should God's protection be for the people brought and paid for by the blood of Jesus? The folks in the Old Testament were not born again; because Jesus had not gone to the cross and died for our sins yet. We are not only born again, but are blood washed, Blood bought by the Son, and God the Holy Spirit. The Word of God is open to all that will seek it! You will, know that you know, that you know that God is real and that He wants to fellowship with you. Again, your security was purchased at the cross 2000 years ago. Why don't you claim what belongs to you?

Chapter Seventeen

POWs in the Body of Christ

In God there is understanding and strength. If all the understanding and strength you will ever need is in the Lord, why do you look for understanding and strength within yourself, and within other men?

The maker of the Heavens and earth will give you all the understanding and strength you will ever need. God has promised that He will speak, excellent things; right things. In life, there are many roads to travel. With God directing your path, you will never get on the wrong road of life. When you come to the road in marriage.

If God is directing your path, because you fear the Lord, you will not take the wrong (wife) path of marriage. If God is directing your path you will not take the wrong (husband) path in marriage. On path of job, if God is directing your job path, because you fear the Lord with all heart, you will not take the wrong (job) path and never enjoy what you are doing.

The fear (awe or respect) of Lord takes into account a wide arrangement of your life. Every aspect of your life is affected by whether or not you fear the Lord. In the Body of Christ, this is a very serious subject. Many of God's Children are held captive in the Body of Christ by the devil. One of the devil's favorite tools is the tool of tradition.

You may have grown up in a church were they did not teach on healing. So the devil puts a sickness on you and you accept it. According to the Word of God, Jesus bore are sickness and diseases on the cross. Every year this country prepares for the flu. Why? I can answer that question— no revelation of the Word of God. Christians line up to get a flu shot, when the Great Physician has the cure to all of our sickness and diseases. Who are you that are lining up for the flu shots—POWs in the Body of Christ? We believe that a flu shot is necessary to keep from getting the flu.

He personally bore our sins in His (own) body on the tree (as on an altar and offered Himself on it), that we might die (cease to exist) to sin and live to righteousness. By His wounds you have been healed (1 Pet. 2:24).

If you are healed, then you are not sick. If you are healed, you do not have a disease. The flu is a disease that is loose in the world. You brothers or sisters are not part of the world. The Scriptures say we are living in the world, but we are not part of the world. Your home is Heaven, and you live in the Kingdom of God.

What you do not recognize is that you live in two kingdoms at the same time. When you are born into this world, you are born into the Kingdom of this world (physically) and when you are born again, you are supernaturally born into the Kingdom of God (spiritually).

You must recognize that God is your source for all your needs you are to seek God and not man. God gave a seed (Jesus) in order to get a harvest (you and me). We are part of the Family of God.

But seek (aim at and strive after) first of all His Kingdom and His righteousness (His way of doing and being right), and then all these things taken together will be given you besides (Matt. 6:33).

Why did God make this statement! Because we live in this world, but we are not part of this world, when it comes to getting things that this world needs to survive. If we follow God's principles, we will never need for anything. The problem is, we do not follow God's principle, but the world's principle, therefore, come under attack of the devil and are taken prisoner of war even though we are in the Body of Christ.

Only about twenty percent of the Body of Christ are tithers! God says you are a robber if you do not tithe. You are robbing God of what already belongs to Him and also robbing Him of the opportunity to bless you. God asks for the first ten percent of your gross salary, not what you think you should give Him. Not ten percent of your net salary, but ten percent of your gross salary. If you are not tithing, you are a POW in the Body of Christ. Think about that for a moment! A POW does not have the same rights as someone that is not a POW. A POW is limited in what they eat and where they go. They must answer to someone who is not normally in their Chain of Command. You stop God, by not tithing, from being the Commander In Chief of your life. In the Book of Malachi it is put so gracefully; Malachi 3:8-9 says:

Will a man rob or defraud God? Yet you rob and defraud Me. But you say, In what way do we rob or defraud You? (You have withheld your) tithes and offerings. You are cursed with the curse, for you are robbing Me, even this whole nation.

What right then do you have to ask God to help you to get your son or daughter off of drugs?. God loves us, but He is a Holy God and has put into action a law of sowing and reaping. If you are sowing robbery then you will reap robbery.

Now can you understand why things do not happened for you? Check out the curse that you have cursed yourself with if you are not tithing. Satan has POWs in the world too, but there is not any reason for POWs to exist in the Body of Christ. You do not have to stay in the POW camp, you can escape to freedom.

The escape route is the Word of God! Study the Word of God so you can know the promises of God that belong to you. Why do we have POWs in the Body of Christ? People do not know the promises of God that belong to them. God does not want you to be sick or broke. God wants you to bring glory to Him. A sick or broke Christian does not bring glory to God.

Here is where that tool of tradition comes into play: "God put this sickness on me to show me something." I am sorry sister or brother, but can you tell me one thing? How can God put sickness on you when Jesus took all sickness and diseases in His Body so you would not have to take it in your body?

If Jesus took sickness and diseases in His Body then they do not belong to me, and when they try to come on me, which they will, I have a Name that is above every name that will cause anything to leave my body—the name of Jesus.

Believe the Word of God, for it is the power to salvation! Jesus gave us His Name to use. In a court of law that term is Power of Attorney. When someone gives you the Power of Attorney, you are acting on behalf of that person. So whatever rights that person has belong to you while you are acting on their behalf. We have the same rights against the devil that Jesus had.

Get this—Jesus defeated the devil. If Jesus defeated the devil, we defeated the devil, and do not have to take any stuff off of him. The Word of God says the devil is a spoiled and defeated foe. I beseech you brother and sister, take your appointed place in the Body of Christ and speak the Word to claim all of the promises of God that belong to you.

God did not give his seed (Jesus) to get the harvest (you and me) for nothing. We are to go forth like Caleb and claim our mountain (Num. 13). When Israel was trying to possess the promised land, twelve went forward to spy out the land. Ten became POWs of the circumstances and two did not. The names of the two who did not become POWs of the circumstances are written in the Bible, but you do not know the names of the ten that became POWs of the circumstances. Why? A loser is never glorified. God will always glorify a winner.

You must remember that you do not belong to the kingdom of darkness. You belong to the Kingdom of God, purchased by the blood of Jesus Christ, our Lord and Savior.

Another category of POWs in the Body of Christ is marriage! Christian marriages, that are supposed to last forever, are ending in divorce at the the same rate that marriages in the world end. What's up? We are supposed to be a light to the world. What does that mean? I believe when the world looks to the marriages of the Body of Christ they are supposed to see a light of love and joy and not of hate and divorce.

The world is to look to the Church for guidance in all areas. If the children of the Kingdom of God are divorcing as fast as the children of the world who can they look to? Why are we divorcing as fast as the children of the world? Many are POWs in this area. They will not work things out like the Word says or take counseling from anointed men or women of God. They go to the ungodly for counseling and reap what they sow. Godly counseling produced godly results and ungodly counseling produces ungodly results.

If you are an eagle then why are you going to the chickens for advice? They also are not seeking God in the situation. We must understand that marriage must be founded upon the Word of God. It must be built upon a proper relationship between the marriage partners and with God. For a marriage to work, it must be founded upon the Word of God. It cannot be built on feelings, hopes, or dreams.

We are in a battle the moment we are born into this world. Remember this we are in a battle! Who side are you on God's or the devil's? You can be born again, spirited filled and still be a POW. Why? If you do not know the Word of God; the devil will try to keep you off track and in the camp of the POW of the Body of Christ. The troops that are not POWs hear more information then those held captive.

If your marriage is in trouble do not become a POW. Claim the promises of God. Proverbs 15:1, says: A soft answer turns away wrath, but grievous words stirs up anger. Proverbs 11:29, says, He who troubles his own house shall inherit the wind, and the foolish shall be servant to the wise of heart.

Both of these Scriptures are promises of God that can be used in your marriage. Speak the Word! I hate religion, but I love a relationship with God. If we speak God's Word to Him, we are guaranteed an answer from Him. God the Father loves to hear His children speaking His Word to Him, so He can answer. It makes God happy to hear one of His own children speak His Word to Him. Be specific when you speak His Word. The Word says you have not because you don't ask! When Jesus was about to be crucified, He said something to Pilate that each Christian today should review. It was this: Therefore Pilate said to Him, "So You are a king?" Jesus answered, "You say correctly that I am a king. For this I have been born, and for this I have come into the world, to testify to the truth. Everyone who is of the truth hears My voice" (John 18:37).

If you are of the truth, you will hear the voice of the Lord and come out of the POW camp and into the Lord's camp. Pilate asked Jesus to tell him the truth. The truth is found in the Word of God.

There are Air Force Regulations governing instructions on how to accomplish each phase of your job. In the Body of Christ there are governing instructions on how to accomplish each phase of your Christian life—the Bible.

In The Air Force, if you do not follow the instructions laid out in the Air Force Regulations, you could lose out on career options. In The Body of Christ, if you do not follow the Word of God you could, and will, lose out on the promises of God that are open to all members of The Body of Christ.

Suppose Miss Bucketmouth has been talking about you and another mouth tells you about it. What is your godly response? Forgiveness! If you say that you can't forgive, you have just let yourself get into the POW camp of unforgiveness.

Now let's say that your best friend calls you and wants you to pray for her son who is wrapped tight in a cult. Your friend knows that when two agree there is power in prayer. Many members of this cult have already killed themselves, and many are planning on accomplishing the job.

You can't help your friend if you are in unforgiveness, because when the truth is told, you are a POW in the Body of Christ. Jesus said if you would not forgive your Father in Heaven will not forgive you. So when you come into agreement with your friend, only her prayers are answered by the Father. Your half of the prayer could have been the part that would break your friend's son free of that cult. Instead, you find out that your friend's son killed himself.

Can you see the seriousness of being a POW in the Body of Christ? You made yourself a POW because you would not forgive. You position yourself with the devil and allowed him to take you into the prisoner of war camp even those you are in the Body of Christ. We are all soldiers in The Army of the Lord!

You can come to church each Sunday, but in reality you are a POW. You are not as effective as those who enjoy complete freedom from the POW camps. You are an unemployed soldier who is a POW in the Body of Christ. Your prayers are not as effective as others, you do not get breakthroughs like others; you find sickness coming upon you regularly.

Why? Unbeknown to you, the devil has you in the POW camp, because of your disobedience to the Word of God. The devil has two POW camps, one with Christians and one with his people. His people have only one way out—Jesus! Christians have only one way out— obedience to The Word of God!

Jesus was obedient to the Father in all that He did. We are to follow His example and be obedient to the Father while we are on this earth. How do you obtain obedience in your life—speaking the Word of God. If you speak what the Word of God says about yourself, victory must come. God's promises never fail! Find out what the Word of God says about you and start confessing it over you and your family today.

Tradition has held many in the POW camp. My mother or father did not do it like that. In the church that I attended while I grew up, the service lasted only one hour. I thought that they were crazy, because they were speaking in tongues. All of this has brought me to one thing—I knew of God, but I did not know God.

There is a difference between knowing of someone and knowing someone. Tradition in the Body of Christ has caused many of the members to know of God, but not know God. I received the Holy Spirit when I was born again. When you are born again, you go from an unbeliever to a believer. The Holy Spirit is the one that helps you into the Body of Christ, but there is also the baptism of The Holy Spirit or receiving of the Holy Spirit.

Paul, on one of his journeys came across some of John the Baptists disciples and asked an important question to them. Have you received the Holy Spirit since you believed?

I could ask you the same. You were birthed out of the kingdom of darkness into the Kingdom of God's dear Son by the Holy Spirit. To receive the baptism of the Holy Spirit, Luke 11:13 says you must ask Him!

One of the gifts of the Holy Spirit is speaking in other tongues. There is a reason that God gives this gift. As a parent why do you give gifts to your children? You love them. God the Father is not any different, He loves us.

Jude 20 tells us why He gave us other tongues. But you, beloved, build yourselves up (founded) on your most holy faith (make progress, rise like an edifice higher and higher), praying in the Holy Spirit.

If you will not believe the Word of God and ask God for the infilling or baptism of the Holy Spirit, then I must say one thing to you: The POW camp of tradition is holding you tight. It might be tight but it is right! I did not write any of the Bible, but I do believe it with all of my heart.

I did not know about speaking with other tongues. I was raised up part Baptist and part Holiness. I had never heard anyone speak or teach on the Baptism of the Holy Spirit until I came to Sacramento, California. I did not realize I was a POW in the area of the baptism of the Holy Spirit until after I received the baptism, and was set free. I am on an assignment to set as many free as I can through the blood of Jesus and the Power of The Holy Spirit. I was never asked to accept Jesus as my Lord and Savior until I was thirty-two-years-old.

Unfortunately, there were many POWs in my path growing up. The Word of God says to study to show yourself approved unto God. I was a POW in the area of tithing before I arrived in Sacramento, California, because no one taught me about tithing. What's so sad is that I was under the curse and did not know it. Like a lot of you who are reading this book—you can only advance as far as the knowledge you get. Many, and I mean many of you are POWs and do not know it.

Ask God Almighty through His Holy Spirit to reveal to you what areas you have allowed the devil to take you captive an make you a POW because of your lack of knowledge. God also says that His people perish for a lack of knowledge! I am not trying to put anyone down, but to help you get all that God has for you.

God is using anointed men and women around this world to set His people free. He is tried of you being in Egypt and in bondage. His Son paid the price already to set you free. If only one person gets the revelation of this book, that one person can set thousands free. God wants you to take your rightful place in His Kingdom. Too many of us are out of place!

Another subject comes to mind: women teaching or pastoring! Paul in one of his writings was calling on a woman who was the leader of the church in her house. When Paul wrote the letter, he was dealing with the married women who were not leaders of the church in their homes. He was instructing them on the correct behavior of a wife. Again we have accepted tradition handed down not the Word of God, but the word of men. Granted Paul was a man, but like all those who wrote the Bible, he was a man used by the Holy Spirit. The Holy Spirit is the author of Paul's letters, Paul is the coauthor. Like other books of the Bible, the Holy Spirit is the author.

God used women to bring across His Word too. In fact, age or gender are not factors that concern God, the heart is the telling factor for God. Paul received the Holy Spirit and was never the same! Check it out, when he was Saul, he killed Christians, but when God changed him, God changed his name to Paul and he became the greatest Christian to ever live.

Paul was very much into tradition and knew of God, but did not know God. It was not until he met Jesus and received the baptism of the Holy Spirit that Paul walked out of the doors of the POW camp of tradition. Tradition caused a nation to kill Jesus! The nation of Israel is still in the POW camp of tradition, but God's love for this Nation has never ended. God still loves Israel today!

The United States of America has prospered as a nation because it has helped the nation of Israel. God says that He would bless those who bless the nation of Israel. What POW camp are you in? The Lord Our God does not like the fact that you are in a POW camp; He wants you free from every thing that would stop you from receiving the full blessings of Him. How many of you reading this book know God?

Think of what it means to know a person. You spend time with that person. In order to know God, you must spend time with Him. You must worship Him everyday, and wait on Him to lead you through His Holy Spirit.

I challenge you to start today having a meaningful relationship with the Holy Spirit and God the Father, God the Son. Only the Holy Spirit can tell you what areas of your spiritual life that you have become a POW.

Another area where many fail is in regard to the Bible. I believe what the Bible says, though I did not write it. Any issue that you may have, you must take up with God. If you will believe the Word of God, you will be set free from the bondage of the devil (POW Camps).

Finances are a big one! God is never trying to take any thing from you, He is always trying to get something to you. Think about this for a moment: Abraham was rich, David was rich, Solomon was also rich. All these men were servants of the Most High God.

We are of the seed of Abraham. We were grafted into the family of God so that the blessings of Abraham would come upon us. God made Abraham rich because of his obedience and He will do the same for us if we are obedient. I would go as far to say that three-fourths of the Body of Christ are POWs in the area of finances. They are held captive by the devil to keep them from establishing God's covenant upon the earth.

We are having bake sales, when God has said, He will give us the power to get wealth to establish

His covenant upon the earth. Come out! The Word of God says to come out among them and entered no more. We are not to be a POW, but a warrior in the army of Christ. Take your rightful place in the Army of the Lord. We are to be the head and not the tail, above only, and not beneath.

Chapter Eighteen

The Fear of the Lord

What is the fear of the Lord? God, speaking in Jeremiah 4:22, says:

For my people are foolish, They have not known me. They are silly children, and they have no understanding. They are wise to do evil, but to do good they have no knowledge.

Each person who has the fear of the Lord in them are blessed. Examples of some of the people who had the fear of the Lord upon them were: Noah (Heb. 11:7); Abraham (Gen. 22:12); Jacob (Gen. 28:16- 17); Joseph (Gen. 42:18); David (Ps. 57;) Obadiah (1 Kings 18:12); Job (Job 1:8); Nehemiah (Neh. 5-15); Early Christians (Acts 9:31). These men were empowered with the ability of God to get the job done. Each and every one, including the Early Christians, ended up blessed—not only spiritually, but materially. Abraham was called the richest man of his time as well as David. Another Scripture that fitted these men is Proverbs 8:34, says Blessed is the man who listens to me.

This fear of the Lord is an awe, or respect for the Lord. I was a young boy who struggled in school. I graduated, but was not on anyone's honor roll. I did not know who I really was. All of this changed when I received the infilling of the Holy Spirit of God.

I believe the Holy Spirit brings you into an awareness of the fear (awe) of the Lord. Without Him, I do not think you have a clear revelation of the fear of the Lord. Look around at the many churches that do not believe in the infilling of the Holy Spirit, A lot of people in the Body of Christ do not have the fear (awe or respect) of the Lord in their place.

The fear of the Lord is the beginning of wisdom. Let's look at this last statement. If you do not respect someone; you can't receive from that person, even if that person is trying to give something to you, it would be impossible for you to receive from them, because you don't respect them. God the Father is always trying to get something to us, but if we do not have a proper respect for Him we can't receive. If we ask God for His wisdom, but we do not respect Him, it is impossible for us to receive.

Can you see why many churches in America do not show forth the glory of God? They have gone from respecting God, to respecting themselves. God wants us to honor Him and He will see that you received honor. If you fear (awe and respect) the Lord you will keep His ways, not your own. Where is wisdom? With the Lord! If you do not go to Him because you do not fear Him, He cannot give you the wisdom for an successful life. A life that overcomes every area in your life.

Why do people in the Body of Christ have just as much divorces as the world? Lack of wisdom! Many of our brothers and sisters have married spouses that they were not supposed to. There's no wonder that the world is divorce city—they do not have the wisdom of God! We do have and can receive the wisdom of God!

Earlier, we looked at our rights. The wisdom of God is a right that every believer is entitled to. I do not want to offend anyone, but without the wisdom of God, you do not stand a chance in your marriage. The devil is working overtime to destroy marriages, because they represent a covenant relationship. He hates marriages and all those who enter into them. It does not matter to him were you are located. All that matters to him is that he can get to you and cause strife and confusion.

If you fear the Lord you will follow His Word. His Word doesn't give the right to divorce except for adultery, all things being equal. If you apply the wisdom of God and the love of God to your marriage, and invite Jesus into your marriage, you have divorce-proofed your marriage.

The Strong's definition for wisdom—knowledge guided by understanding.

Proverbs 9:10, says; The fear of the Lord is the beginning of wisdom, And the knowledge of the Holy One is understanding. Think about the definition of wisdom for one moment: knowledge guided by understanding. Whose knowledge is guided? It is man's. By whose understanding? It is God's. God takes our knowledge and guides it by His understanding. That is how you can divorceproof your marriage. Allow God to used your knowledge with His understanding to make every decision in your marriage. Make sure that each and every decision made by you and your spouse will be successful. You can't go wrong with God on your side. The fear of the Lord is to respect the Lord and allow Him to make the decisions in your life.

As believers, there is no excuse for not having the wisdom of God operating in your life. If you respect someone you will allow them to give you instructions for life. All God wants is for us to come to Him. He said, we can pray for wisdom (Col. 1:9); if we lack wisdom, we can ask for it (Jas. 1:5).

What is the value of wisdom? According to Proverbs 3:13, wisdom will give us happiness. According to Proverbs 5:16, wisdom will keep us from evil. According to Proverbs 8:11, wisdom is better than rubies. According to Proverbs 16:16 wisdom is above gold in value. According to Ecclesiastes 7:12, wisdom gives life. According to Ecclesiastes 7:19, wisdom makes us strong. According to Ecclesiastes 9:18, wisdom is better than weapons. According to Isaiah 33:6, wisdom insures stability in your life. According to James 3:17, wisdom produces good fruit in your life. Lastly, wisdom produces blessing and favor in your life.

If you fear (awe or respect) the Lord, you are on track for wisdom to flow in every area of your life. Do not take an attitude that wants to be independent of the Lord. Do not do anything without the guided understanding from the Lord. If you will allow yourself to take on this attitude, there will not be anything that you cannot do or have. Why? Because you are out of the way and El Elyon is directing your footsteps. When El Elyon (The Most High God) is directing your footsteps, each footstep hits the direct path of life. You do not waver to the left or to the right. You stay straight on the path of righteousness. You will not miss a step!

How can this be accomplished? By the fear of the Lord. It is the only way you can make sure that you are walking in the plan and purpose God has for your life. If you want to know that you know that you are walking in the plan and purpose for your life, just start to fear (awe or respect) the Lord and see what happens.

Wisdom on how to handle your kids will come to you. Wisdom on what to wear to work or school that day will come to you. Wisdom on what ministry you should be commit to will come to you. Wisdom on who to date and who not to date will come to you. Wisdom on what classes to take in High School or College will come to you. Wisdom on what business to start will come to you. Wisdom on how to be a better husband or wife will come to you.

The fear of the Lord will make you look smart. Why? Because wisdom comes to you, which is your knowledge guided by God's understanding. Whatever the situation; it has got to get in line, when our knowledge is guided by God, understanding shows up.

Can you see why the devil will try all that he knows how to keep a Christian from asking for the wisdom of God or from fearing the Lord? If you have escaped from the kingdom of darkness, he does not want you to hook up with God. How can you hook up with God? By fearing Him.

Wisdom begins when you start to fear the Lord. When you start to fear the Lord; you will start to ask of the Lord. When you start to ask of the Lord, you will receive of the Lord. What will you receive? Wisdom!

If wisdom is knowledge guided by understanding, you and I need to ask for it. If you are not asking for Wisdom, what do you have? Knowledge that is not guided by understanding. Other words you do not have the understanding to apply to the knowledge for the perfect decision to be formed. Why? Your decisions are a shot in the dark, some hit their mark, some miss their mark. Look at life, that is just what takes place in the lives of many Christians. Why? Because they have never come into the revelation of the fear of the Lord in their lives. Without this major issue settled in your life; your Christian walk will be fifty-fifty. Sometimes you will hit the mark, but sometimes you will miss the mark. Does this sound like God's best for your life? If you do not understand something; you cannot make proper decisions.

The devil wants you to think that you can make correct decisions without the Lord. Once you have taken the bait, your correct decision turns into a wrong decision. Think about what the devil told Eve. He tells us the same thing, he told Eve. His reason, to get us to challenge God's authority. If we are not hooked up with God, our knowledge is not guided by God's understanding.

Look at any major city in the United States of America. You will see more homeless people on the streets of America than ever before. Why? Their knowledge is not guided by God's understanding. You can say they fear the Lord, but do they truly fear the Lord? You might know some who you think fears the Lord, but I want to challenge you. Fear is the awe or respect of someone. Most of the people on the streets here in Sacramento, California do not respect or awe the Lord. They are thinking of self and only self. They have made themselves god and have not allowed God to help them.

I am not trying being hard on them or cruel. I love helping them, but I know they do not respect the Lord like they should. Do you respect the Lord like you should? If you do, then you will not steal, cheat, gossip, or backbite. Why? Because God gave us commandments saying we would not do these things. If you love the Lord you will not do these things.

Another word for respect is love. I love the Lord, so I do not practice evil. I ask for the wisdom to know how to handle every aspect of my life. The fear of the Lord will bring goodness into your life, and will cause others to experience the same thing—they will see your light and will want to follow your light straight down the path of righteousness. If you fear the Lord, it will bring others into the same fear. People will want to know how you are getting blessed and you will be able to tell them it is because, I fear the Lord with all my heart and soul.

Chapter Nineteen

What is the Prayer

In order to pray, we must know what prayer is. Prayer is a request made to God. You might be thinking, I have made requests unto God and He did not answer me. There are reasons for that. You must examine yourself. Do you have any unforgiveness in your heart? One of the general requirements of prayer is a unforgiving spirit. Matthew 6:14, says; For if you forgive men their trespasses, your Heavenly Father will also forgive you.

I like the simplicity of the Word of God. It is plain that if you do not forgive others of their trespasses, our Heavenly Father will not forgive us. So, if we come to God in prayer without forgiving, the first thing we must do is to forgive whoever you need to forgive before we ask anything of God. The number one requirement is to have a forgiving spirit.

We all know that if we have sin in our lives, God will not answer our prayers. I want to talk about some other areas in our lives which will cause God not to answer our prayers. We all want our prayers to be answered and for God to be pleased with our lives.

The first area I want to examine in our lives is selfishness. James 4:3 says; You ask and do not receive, because you ask amiss, that you may spend it on your pleasures. Why does God want us to be bless? So we can be a blessing to others. I am not saying that God does not want you to have anything, because He does, that is why He tells us to seek both His Kingdom and Righteousness that He can add good blessing to our lives. He wants us to have things.

What is the attitude in which you ask? Check your attitude! Have you asked God for things amiss, that you may spend it on yourself? If you are blessed, its so you can bless others in the Body of Christ as well as those in the world. God gave us wealth to establish His covenant.

You should not be praying a selfish prayer, but a unselfish prayer, that God will bless you so you can be a blessing to the Body of Christ, as well as others in the world. God is a holy God; His people are to be holy. Remember one thing, it is God who gives us wealth to establish His covenant. He already knows if He can trust you with wealth.

If you are not tithing, do not expect God to bless you with one million dollars. Why? Because you are a God-robber! If I am talking to one person that will check their heart for the spirit of selfishness, I consider this book an success: That one person can take it to another person and that person to another. Christianity started one person at a time. Once you have checked your heart, you will not want to allow the spirit of selfishness to remain. Another reason why you are not getting your prayers answered is doubt. James 1:5-7 says: If any of you lacks wisdom, let him ask of God, who gives to all liberally and without reproach, and it will be given to him. But let him ask in faith, with no doubting, for he who doubts is like a wave of the sea driven and tossed by the wind. For let not that man suppose that he will receive anything from the Lord.

If you are doubting, if the Lord is going to do something for you, then you will not receive nothing from the Lord. Doubt robs you of all that God intends for you to have. Doubt waits at the door of prayer and enters when you allow the thought come to you that the Lord ought not to bless you: Me, not me, He can't do this for me, I am not worthy.

Who told you that lie? Wake up! The devil is trying to steal your request to God. If he can get you to doubt, though your words might reach God, the reply won't return from God. You want your request to arrive and return from God. Doubt is one of the weapons the devil uses on Christians.

Perhaps you have been very close in getting your desired breakthrough, but doubt showed up and captured your faith. Are you sick of your breakthroughs not being answered? Get rid of the spirit of doubt.

How do you get rid of the spirit of doubt? By confessing it to God. Doubt is the opposite of faith. It is a sin. What do you do with sin? You confess it to God (1 John 1:9). Selfishness and doubt are both sins that must be confessed to God. God says, He will not only forgive us, but He will forget our sins. When we confess them to God we put ourselves back in right standing with God.

The spirit of doubt wants to replace God. Anything that you allow to replace God, you allow to become number one in your life. If God is not number one when you ask a request of Him, you are asking amiss. If you are doubting when asking a request of God, you have replaced God as number one in your life.

If is a word God used a lot. Why? Because your freedom of choice is not taken away from you by God. He does want you to make the right choice. We can make right choices! The wise and smart choice would be not to doubt.

The Word says you do not receive anything of the Lord when you doubt. Do you believe the word or not? Another choice! I choose to believe the Word of God with all my heart. If God said it, then it is a done deal as far as I am concerned. I believe the Bible is God speaking to mankind. The God of the universe is speaking. Shouldn't we be paying better attention to what He is saying? If He is saying that a man that doubts will not receive anything from Him, then what would a man that does not doubt receive from Him?

God has been speaking to us in His Word for over 2000 years. If we will take the time to study the Bible, we will find out what the will of the Lord is for our lives. If you seek God, you will find God. Every person who has every made God their number one priority have never failed to find Him.

Another area that you must examine yourself is in the area of disobedience. The spirit of disobedience has been around since Satan rebelled against God. In fact, the spirit of disobedience started with Satan. From Satan, this spirit flowed to Adam and Eve. Our first parents were disobedient to God, and as a result, this spirit is in each person born upon this earth today.

Rebellion is a branch, but disobedience is the root. In fact, selfishness and doubt are both branches, but disobedience is the root. If you get rid of the root, the branches will die.

When you come to the Lord in prayer, you must come with the boldness of a lion. Jesus died to give you this boldness. Stand before the Lord with thanksgiving in your heart in prayer. Prayer for a believer should be twenty-four seven! Everything should be taken to the Lord in prayer.

What you are going to have for dinner should be taken to the Lord in prayer. Jesus is Lord over all areas of your life. What you are going to wear to work should be taken to the Lord in prayer.

Jesus and the Father do care about what you wear. You might say Brother James you have gone to far. I beg your pardon, if Jesus is your Lord, you will ask for his help in every area of your life. Don't you think God knows if the dress or suit that you wear today will cause someone to ask you about it? If they ask, it would be a perfect time to give glory to God. God knows everything. He knows the end and the beginning.

It is like this—if you are a parent you have already been were your children are trying to get to. God has been were His children are trying to get to. He already knows your future. Why not let Him lead you into the promised land? Why do you want to stay in Egypt? Israel stayed in the wilderness for forty years because of their disobedience. Don't stay in the wilderness of life for twenty, forty, or sixty years because of the spirit of disobedience; pray yourself out of the wilderness and into the land of milk and honey.

Chapter Twenty

Fellowship with the Father, Son, and Holy Spirit

The information included in this last chapter is very important to your relationship with God. He is God the Father, God the Son, and God the Holy Spirit. You must keep this in mind! He is again: God the Father, God the Son, and God the Holy Spirit. As the Father, He is Love. As the Son, He took our place on the cross. As the Holy Spirit, He brings us to Himself.

If you do not recognize Him in these roles, you can miss out on what He wants to do in your life. For example, God the Father gives an order, God the Son takes the order, God the Holy Spirit cares out the order. But they are all God, and we are to worship and fellowship with God the Father, God the Son, and God the Holy Spirit.

They were all present at the beginning of time. They were all present at the baptism of Jesus by John the Baptist. I do not understand how God can be one, yet function in three persons, but the Bible says He does, so that is good enough for me. If, God said it, then it is true. The subject of this chapter is fellowship with God the Father, God the Son, and God the Holy Spirit.

How do we do that? The word fellowship denotes to spend time with someone. I am talking about not just praying, but talking to them just like you talk to your friends. You talk to God the Father, you talk to God the Son, and you talk to God the Holy Spirit. They are the first, second, and third person of the Godhead. All are to be worshiped! All are to be fellowshipped.

Again, fellowship means to spend time together. We are to spend time with the Father, the Son, and the Holy Spirit. If you spend time with someone you get to know them very well. Men, generally, have a harder time than women spending time with the Godhead. Because you will be required to be still and listen to what God wants to speak to you. It is very important that you give this time to the Godhead, because it is in this time that God tells you what He wants done in your life (purpose for living). God has a plan and a purpose for each person on this earth. It is up to us to find out this plan and purpose.

One of the ways we can find out God's plan and purpose for our lives is in worship and fellowship with the Godhead. You can start off by thanking God for all He has done for you. If you are breathing His air at this moment, He has done something for you. You could be dead! We forget about the goodness of God. He is so merciful to us and we are so unthankful. Many times, we trample the blood of Jesus by our conduct. His Blood was a precious price to pay for mankind. We should be thankful that Jesus went through all He did to bring us back into right standings with God the Father.

If you have not worshiped the Lord today, please start. It is an awesome experience when you set aside yourself and all your problems and give yourself to the Lord in worship. He loves for His children to worship Him in spirit and in truth.

When you spend time with the Lord telling Him how much you love Him you get a high that nothing can change. This high comes from your relationship with the Lord, and it is awesome. I can't tell you how it feels, you must experience it for yourself. It's you and God! The love He has for His children is truly felt in your spirit, soul, and mind. You must experienced what fellowship with the Lord is all about.

No one can know you like Jesus! He is the greatest of all times. Fellowship brings you into awareness of all that God has for you. Start today—spend at least thirty minutes in fellowship with the Lord. Just you and Him in communion like you have never experienced it before. When you are in fellowship with God, you are changed and will never, never, never be the same again. I can say this: God will not change, but you will be changed and will go to the next level of your life.

About the Author

James Henry Lincoln, Sr was born in New Castle, PA. He graduated from New Castle Senior High School. After graduation, he enlisted in the United States Air Force and retired from the United States Air Force in the grade of Master Sergeant. James spent a total of 22 years in the United States Air Force and traveled to such places as Korea, Japan, Okinawa, and Hawaii.

While stationed in the State of Ohio, James underwent a radical transformation when he accepted the Lord Jesus Christ into his life. James went from an arrogant person to a humble person. A man who once only cared about himself, to a person who cares about the welfare of others. Overtaken by the mental illness of his first wife, James reached out for the Lord. James was then transferred from the State of Ohio to the State of California.

After spending three years in the State of California, James was transferred to South Korea for one year. Returning to the State of California after a year in South Korea, James and his first wife were divorced.

On, August 23, 1986, James and Gwendolyn (Palmer) Tyler were married at South Lake Tahoe, California. James did not know it at the time, but Gwendolyn was the answer to a prayer that had taken place some years back: James had prayed to the Lord concerning his first wife's relationship with the Lord.

James' love for the Lord caused him to ask the Lord to give his wife the same love for him that he had. His current wife was this person.

On, April 19,1992, Gwendolyn accepted the Lord Jesus Christ into her life.

She is a woman who loves and seeks the Lord with all of her heart. Exactly what James had prayed for.

James and Gwendolyn blended families and together they had five children. Michael passed away on November 15, 2017 at the age 30. James Jr and Andrew came from James' first marriage and Ava and Anthony from Gwendolyn first marriage. Ava and Anthony were adopted by James when they were young.

All of the remaining children are now adults. James and Gwendolyn have been married for thirty-seven years.

James was called into the ministry of the Gospel as an evangelist teacher in August, 1994, and was licensed as a Minister at Calvary Christian Center on June 7, 1997.

James serves under the leadership of Pastor Phillip G. Goudeaux at Calvary Christian Center in Sacramento, California. James is on his way to being known as a motivational speaker and author who inspires and encourages people to be all that God called them to be.

James also received his Bachelor's Degree in Business Administration and a minor in Management on December 15, 2015.

Resources

The Vines Expository Dictionary. Copyright ©1985 by Thomas Nelson, Inc., Publishers.

A revision of An Expository Dictionary of Biblical Word © 1984 Thomas Nelson, Inc.

A Compilation of Nelson's Expository Dictionary of the Old Testament © 1980 by Thomas Nelson, Inc.

An Expository Dictionary of New Testament Words ©1983, Fourth printing. Published in Nashville, Tennessee, by Thomas Nelson, Inc., Publishers. Distributed in Canada by Lawson Falle, Ltd., Cambridge, Ontario

The New Strong's Exhaustive Concordance of the Bible. © 1990, Thomas Nelson Publishers.

The Merriam Webster's Collegiate Thesaurus. © 1980 by Merriam Webster Inc.

Printed by Libri Plureos GmbH in Hamburg, Germany